NEW MEXICO ODYSSEY

New Mexico
ODYSSEY
TOBY SMITH

University of New Mexico Press
Albuquerque

Library of Congress Cataloging in Publication Data

Smith, Toby, 1946-
 New Mexico odyssey.

 Bibliography: p.
 Includes index.
 1. New Mexico—Social life and customs.
2. New Mexico—History, Local. 3. New Mexico—
Biography. I. Title.
F801.2.S64 1987   978.9   87-5877
ISBN 0-8263-0987-9 (pbk.)

Two essays—"Los Arabes" and "Pavement"—first appeared in *New Mexico Maga-zine*. They are reprinted here in revised version courtesy of the Editor, *New Mexico Magazine*.
All of the other pieces in the book are revised versions of articles from the *Albuquer-que Journal* magazine, "Impact." They are reprinted by permission of the *Albuquer-que Journal*, a copyrighted publication of the Journal Publishing Co.

To Susan, a compass

Contents

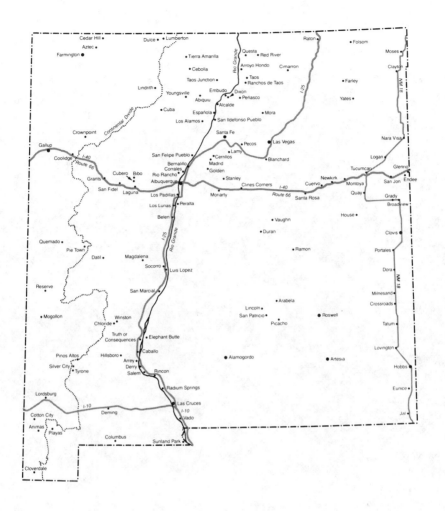

Preface

When I was starting out as a newspaper reporter, a city editor liked to remind me as I left on assignments to "Keep your eyes and ears open." At the time, I dismissed the words as superfluous advice, something along the line of making sure I held my breath underwater. Yet through the writing of the pieces in this book, I've come to understand that often the obvious is worth remembering.

This book is about serendipitous wanderings. When I used my eyes and ears, and sometimes even my nose, on those wanderings, I discovered things about New Mexico that I might have otherwise missed.

An earlier collection of mine entitled *Dateline: New Mexico* focused on the people of the state. *New Mexico Odyssey* is about people, too, but it is more about places—big cities, small towns, rivers, roads, and mountain ranges—and how they can shape a life. Look, for instance, at the inhabitants of little House, New Mexico, a farming community south of Tucumcari. Many House residents hung on through a series of droughts in the 1950s that turned their soil to chalk dust. These are good people, but tough, forged by elements that would break a lesser person. When I asked them questions, all answered with the bull's-eye stare and unembellished words of survivors.

At some New Mexico places discovery was a struggle. Attempting to locate the geographically vague Continental Divide in Hidalgo County can be like searching for a volcano in Mississippi. You roam about in the blistering sun until you've either run out of patience or gasoline. And then when you work up the courage to ask a rawboned rancher where the Continental Divide is, he tells you this: "Son, you're standing on it."

A section of this odyssey is called Trails and it sets the framework for all of the book. Trails across the state led me from southwestern New Mexico's Gray Ranch, one of the biggest spreads in the region, to the fast-blink outpost of Cedar Hill near Farmington. Trails took me from the plain lobby of an ancient movie theater in Clayton, to the fancy back seat of a limousine in Albuquerque; from the wet raft ride on the Rio Grande near Taos, to the dry oil patch in Lea County; from the young, promising new company town named Playas, to the old, time-worn mountain village of Peñasco.

Taking the right trail was vital. When writer Paul Theroux embarked on a walking tour of the coast of England, he said, "My route was crucial. It was the most important aspect of travel. In choosing a route, one was choosing a subject."

As I chose my routes, and thus my subjects, I was struck by how the New Mexico landscape can lead a traveler to points of common reference in uncommon places. In the Lincoln County hamlet of San Patricio, I met the family of artist Peter Hurd, and many subjects Hurd painted. In Ramon, seventy miles to the north of San Patricio, and the site of another story, I paused at a filling station Hurd once painted. During a third outing, in Logan, 130 miles northeast of Ramon, I stumbled upon the wall of a motel that an ex-Hurd student had turned into a mural. Two small places, Datil and Otowi Bridge, on two different trails 230 miles apart, each helped to produce a notable book of New Mexico nonfiction.

Occasionally, the odyssey took me in circles. When I tried locating a home in Albuquerque's Northeast Heights, made famous in a 1958 photograph, I spent nearly two weeks checking maps and old city directories, and scouting neighborhoods by car. When I finally found the house on Muriel Street, I realized I had been jogging past the rear of it for several years.

Often luck was involved, no matter what trail I chose. The morning I set off to do a story on Pie Town, I worried about where to begin. Then, a casual remark in a Catron County cafe gained me a personalized tour of a place with a polychromatic past and name.

Some people, my children mainly, frequently asked me when I

returned from wandering, what had I brought back. A good story, I hope, I usually answered. J. Frank Dobie, a Texan who periodically crossed into New Mexico in search of tales, once wrote to his wife that he wouldn't return home until he got what he wanted: drama, romance, and mental pictures of a place nobody could forget. From time to time, however, I have retrieved objects, and that is part of the satisfaction of any odyssey. In Portales I secured a bag of Valencia peanuts harvested along Highway 18. From a lonely railroad siding near Las Vegas I picked up among the cinders a rusted but perfectly formed spike. Even in Albuquerque, my hometown, I did not return empty-handed. Jack Rittenhouse, a jewel of a man who lives just off Central Avenue, gifted me with a copy of a priceless guidebook to Route 66 that he'd written in 1946.

I met a lot of old-timers on the trail—ex-Harvey Girls, weather-beaten cowpunchers, a homesteader just shy of ninety. I often sought them out, in fact, for what better way to find out about a place than to talk to someone who has spent seven or eight decades around it? Yet I often learned from young people, too. When I asked a student attending a celebrated underground elementary school in Artesia what he thought about sitting in a classroom that didn't have any windows, he glanced at me for a second, then said, "If there were windows here, I wouldn't be able to see out of them."

Curiously perhaps, the New Mexico place I feel most comfortable in is the east side, a part of the state seldom pictured in travel brochures. Some of the most generous people on earth live there. Sure, it's flat as a flapjack, but most of those people who call the east side home know what they have. I found it one morning driving north of Clovis. As a marigold-colored sun poked up, I watched windmills spin lazily, heard the steady *swoosh* of giant field sprinklers, and inhaled the sweet scent of freshly cut wheat. That is one trail I want to take again.

Any writer who lets a publisher gather his words between two pieces of cardboard, with some of those words being the pronoun I, takes a large risk. Former *New York Times* journalist Gloria Emerson, who has followed stories to Central America, Ireland, and Vietnam, among other locales, often puts herself in her articles. In fact, she frequently cannot separate herself from her subjects. I asked her about it once. She explained that, yes, her objectivity is possibly diminished when she does this. But she also said her beliefs in the people she meets and the places she writes about, is enlarged. And so is the reader's.

This is a travel book then, and I am a part of it. But the star is New Mexico and it shines for the reader only. I'm simply an enlarger, an observer reporting what he has seen and heard and could not forget.

Coincidentally, one of my favorite travel writers happens to be a man closely identified with New Mexico. A little more than 100 years ago, Charles F. Lummis took a hike across the United States. *A Tramp Across the Continent* is Lummis's account of his enterprising and daring trek. On my odyssey through New Mexico, mostly accomplished in a four-wheel drive vehicle, I often tried to imagine Lummis, in wild and desolate lands, on foot. It was difficult.

Traveling a circuitous route, the twenty-six-year-old Lummis left Ohio to traverse eight states and territories in 143 days. He frequently covered thirty to forty miles a day. Awaiting him in California was the job of city editor of the *Los Angeles Times*. En route to that post Lummis filed stories to the *Times* describing his adventures. Lummis took the hike, he admitted, "for pure pleasure." Iconoclastic, combative, and immensely cocky, Lummis walked for the "joy of living outside the sorry fences of society." His words also helped readers see this country in ways that had never been done before.

Lummis devotes half of *A Tramp Across the Continent* to New Mexico. In Santa Fe he encounters sinister politicians; near Tijeras he eats chile for the first time. He lives among Isleta Pueblo and Navajo Indians. Some of Lummis's stories are hard to swallow. Because he traveled alone, no one could verify his shooting a wildcat at 200 yards, or disarming desperadoes time and again. However, when Lummis leaves New Mexico, toward the end of the book, and says he is genuinely sad, the reader is sad, too. Ten decades later, the goal of *A Tramp Across the Continent*—one man's search for a purpose in life, a *place*—remains clear because Lummis kept his eyes and ears open.

Most of the stories in this book appeared in the *Albuquerque Journal*. Some turned up first in *New Mexico Magazine*. I wish to thank the editors of both of those publications for letting me wander and for letting me reprint what I found. The duration of a newspaper or magazine article is ephemeral, often shorter than the lifespan of a mayfly. I am grateful to the University of New Mexico Press for encouraging the resuscitation of these pieces, and for helping to breathe fresh oxygen into them. Most of all I am grateful to New Mexico, a state that offers the alert traveler continual surprises. Any wrong turns I have made along the way are no one's fault but mine.

In Spanish there is a word for which I can't find a counterword in English. It is the verb vacilar, *present participle* vacilando. *It does not mean vacilating at all. If one is vacilando, he is going somewhere but doesn't greatly care whether he gets there, although he has direction.*

—*John Steinbeck*
Travels with Charley

I

Memories

Those Harvey Girls

For the record, they were waitresses—but not of the coffee-tea-or-me persuasion. Heavens no. They worked for what was once the biggest but most virtuous restaurant chain in the country. Thirty years ago, the Fred Harvey Company was a $30 million-a-year business, with 6,000 employees, 55 eateries, 12 resort hotels and 100 railroad dining cars.

Except in scattered names, the firm no longer survives. When the railroad was king, Fred Harvey was a major part of the monarchy. When the railroad began to vanish, so did the Harvey name. Harvey's story has been recounted before: a British lad who came to the United States with barely a dime, ambitious Fred rapidly built an empire of good eating. He opened his first Harvey House in St. Louis, Missouri, in 1859, then one in Topeka, Kansas, then one farther west.

In those days, when railroads did not have dining cars, Harvey had a better idea: he would provide superb food and rooms at train stations en route. To serve passengers and railroad men, young women were recruited from the East and Midwest. They were given housing and looked after as carefully as boarding-school students. They were called Harvey Girls.

Many Harvey Girls were former schoolmarms. All were upright and moral, or so the story went. This chaste trait was epitomized in the 1946 Judy Garland movie musical, *The Harvey Girls*. (A trivia tip: the film featured the rousing song "Atchison, Topeka and Santa Fe.")

Early in this century, there were more than 100 Harvey Houses, the majority of them in the Southwest and West. In New Mexico, at least a dozen Harvey Houses flourished. In most towns, the Harvey House was the social hub.

Harvey Girls weren't paid extravagantly, but the benefits were good. Will Rogers once said Fred Harvey and his girls "kept the West in food and wives." Legend has it that 20,000 of the handmaidens wound up as brides to ranchers, cowboys, and railroaders.

There exists no Society for the Preservation of Former Harvey Girls, but perhaps there should. To listen to an ex-Harvey Girl talk of her work is to feast on a sumptuous slice of social history.

So now meet Neva, Opal, and Pearl, three women who found their destiny—and husband—out west as a Harvey Girl. The trio live in Albuquerque and their combined age is greater than 250 years. They live in their memories, too, which are faded at times, but important enough not to be forgotten.

Neva Davis

I'm not going to remember a lot of this, dear, because I'm ninety-one years old. But here goes.

I started out wanting to be a beautician, a manicurist, guess you'd say. This was back in Anthony, Kansas, in the southwestern part of that state. I was one of seven children. After a while I went to work in a hotel there. No, I don't recall the name of it. Later, I went to a Harvey House somewhere south of Fort Worth, Texas. I stayed there six months. Do you know what happened to a Harvey Girl after she worked six months? They gave her a round-trip ticket home and a month's vacation.

After Fort Worth—this was during World War I—I came over to Clovis to visit my sister, May McFarland. She passed away a long time ago. May was one of the ones who told me to go to Albuquerque. So that's what I did in 1923. I came to the Alvarado Hotel. I had my old trunk with me, and the manager said he'd bring it right up on the second floor where there was a dormitory. So I had a job. We stayed two to a room at the Alvarado, us Harvey Girls. It was a plain room, really just two single beds and a dresser. There was hardly space for my old trunk.

Miss Jenny was our hostess and she was very strict. We had to
have proper etiquette in the dining room. I liked working the coffee
shop better. In the coffee shop customers would ask for your station,
the place where you worked. I had lots of friends ask for my station.
Oh yes, we had rules. A Harvey Girl had better get in before a speci-
fied hour or the back door was locked. Some girls would try to climb
over the fence to get in on time. They could be rough on the girls.
Once a girl married a fellow who worked in the kitchen, and they
fired them both. I could never understand that.

What did people eat? Well, Fred Harvey pie. And lots of coffee,
of course. I'm a vegetarian and most everybody else were meat eat-
ers. I didn't like to work the counter because the railroad men who
ate there were always in a rush. Look at this, dear. It's a 1945 menu
I've saved from the Alvarado. See. Salmon steak dinner for one dollar. Isn't that something?

You earned your money in tips. Nobody got any overtime. In
the early days, everybody tipped a dime. There were little pockets in
your uniform to put the tips. Once Bob Hope came in alone to the
Alvarado and ordered a sirloin steak. Tipped me fifty cents. That was
generous. People didn't pay attention to the percentage thing, though.
They tipped you whatever they had.

What I loved about being a Harvey Girl was the comradeship.
We had so much fun living in the dormitory—me, and Effie Jenks,
Edith Haselton, and the rest. Gladys Bronson was studying ballet and
she would try to teach it to everybody up there. At Christmas time,
we had a tree set up and some of the men downtown would ask to
come up to see it. Some of the girls would try to imitate the customers, especially the picky ones.

I always liked the families with children; guess that's because I
never had any children of my own. I was married to Harry Davis—he
died sometime in the 1940s. I met him in the Alvarado's kitchen.
For a while we had a chicken ranch out on North Edith.

No, I never did meet anybody I didn't like. Oh, once during
the war we could only serve so much bread to each customer and
one couple wanted to take home extra rolls. There was quite a fuss
about that.

Being a Harvey Girl was no disgrace. Far from it. I was doing my
bit to the best of my ability. I retired in 1959, and I miss it. I get
Social Security and some railroad retirement, but I'm able to live nice
because I made some money in the stock market.

Oh, goodness no, I don't know where my uniforms are. I've moved so many times. I bet I could get in them, though. I weighed 135 pounds back then. I weigh 114 now.

Opal Hill

First thing you must understand is that the Fred Harvey organization was no greasy spoon. We used linen from England, tables had to be set just right. If you had a knife out of line, they sent you off the floor.

I was twenty-five when I joined up. This was 1924. Forty-five years later I was still a Harvey Girl. I worked three years before anyone put in a complaint against me: man said his steak wasn't done right.

Originally, I was a secretary. After graduating from the Metropolitan Business College in Dallas, Texas, I took a job with a bonding company in Little Rock, Arkansas. My first day there the boss asked me out to eat. Second day he asked me to be his sweetheart. I wanted none of that so I went back to Amarillo, Texas.

The Harvey people in Amarillo were looking for nice, clean waitresses. I talked to Mr. Lindsey. He said I was the first girl who came in in six months who wasn't chewing gum. I was at the Harvey House in Amarillo for three years. I started out wearing badge number fourteen. You see, in the Harvey organization, all the girls wore badges on the top left of their uniform. It was a seniority system. By the time I left Amarillo my badge number was one and I was training girls.

After Texas, I went to Hutchinson, Kansas, and then to Dodge City. In 1930, the Harvey people asked how I would like to go to Cleveland, Ohio. I said I'd go anywhere to get out of Dodge City. From Cleveland, I went to Chicago and then, in 1941, I came to Albuquerque and the Alvarado.

I loved being a Harvey Girl. Loved everything about it. Fred Harvey was an outfit that could not be beaten. You had pride. You didn't wear earscrews or nail polish. In Amarillo, the housekeeper would check our uniforms to see if they was so many inches off the floor and no more.

The uniform changed over the years. In the very old days they wore bows in the hair and long bibs. We had white Elsie collars that came back from the laundry really starched. That black bow tie you pinned on yourself. Toward the end, it was wine-colored, a one-piece dress with a pinafore apron in front. When Amfac took over Harvey in the late 1960s, everyone was told, "Throw out them Harvey Girl uniforms." And they did. What a shame.

But the Harvey operation was a class operation. Up until about 1935, a fellow couldn't eat in the dining room unless he wore a coat. If you didn't have one, we had a bunch of little alpaca jackets we'd hand out. I remember I gave a coat to one fella and said this was our rule. He throwed it back in my face.

I married a railroad man. A lot of Harvey Girls did. My husband was a boilermaker. He's been gone a while now. People thought that because the Harvey Girls were way out in the desert that we were, well, easy. That wasn't true. You could see that in that movie starring Judy Garland. What a lovely story.

I waited on lots of famous people: Jack Benny, Will Rogers, Jeanette MacDonald. It was a wonderful life. In 1970, when they tore down the Alvarado Hotel, I went and watched. Cried and cried. I felt ashamed of myself until I looked around and saw other people doing the same thing.

Pearl Ramsey

Some girlfriends told me about the Harvey Girls. I was working in a print shop in Wright County, Missouri, and was just tired of it. This was 1924. I was, what? Twenty-four years old? My, that's a long time ago.

What I did was go up to Springfield, Missouri. When I got there they told me to go up to Kansas City, where a woman interviewed me. I don't even remember her name. Anyway, she said there was a job for me—in New Mexico! Why, I'd hardly been out of Wright County.

Next thing I did was get on a train and get off at San Marcial, New Mexico. San Marcial, you know, was that nice little place flooded out in 1929. In 1923, it was a booming railroad town, a division point on the Santa Fe. San Marcial's Harvey House was two stories high. Right near the station it was. On the first floor was the restaurant. Up above lived the manager and his wife, and about six Harvey Girls.

Now, I had never worked in a restaurant, so some things took getting used to. Like, when the men would come in and say "java." I honestly didn't know that meant coffee.

The dining room had, as I recall, only three tables. Mostly I worked at the big lunch counter. At first I was on a split shift—2:00 P.M. to 10:00 P.M. Then, when the head waitress, Margaret Sampson was her name, got married, I moved up to Margaret's job and worked days. I'd been making a dollar a day at the print shop, so when they told me I would be getting sixty dollars a month as a Harvey Girl, that was something. Actually, I got about ninety dollars a month; they paid my room and board and laundry, which was my uniforms.

I know you want to know about those uniforms. Everybody does. Well, the blouse was black, and then around it we wrapped this big white apron. We were supposed to wear a black dress under the apron, but they didn't make us so usually we wore just a slip. We could wear our own dark shoes, but not high heels, and most wore a hair net. You could use makeup, but nobody did; I need to now.

Let's see. You had to be in by 10:00 P.M. And no late dates. We had to clean our own glasses and they had to sparkle. And of course, the customer was always right.

One of my customers was Albert Fall. You may be too young to remember him, but he was in that Teapot Dome thing. Well, Mr. Fall tipped me ten dollars. I thought I was rich. Another customer was William Ramsey. He worked for the Santa Fe as a telegraph operator. We were married in March 1924. We're still together.

Two months after I got married, my husband transferred to Rincon, New Mexico. You know where that is? Good. They had a Harvey House in Rincon, but my husband didn't want me to work anymore, so I didn't. So really I was a Harvey Girl for only about a year. But it was a good experience. I learned you have to give and take in life. If things aren't just exactly like you want, you don't holler too much.

Did the Harvey Girls have a reputation? Men liked to flirt with them, if that's what you mean. And some of the girls took advantage of coming out West and doing things. But most were nice and respectable. Oh, the manager would call a few on the carpet once in a while.

It's funny, but I have foot trouble now, especially in my left foot. It could be related to my Harvey Girl days; the only time you sat down was to fold napkins or polish silverware. You worked real hard. They held a train until everybody got through eating.

Something else. I wish I had my Harvey Girl uniforms. Just one of them. I suppose it's kind of like men in the service. When you get out, you throw the uniforms away. Years later, you wish you had them back.

A Slice of Life

Pie Town.

Holy meringue, what a name! And it's genuine, too. Not some sobriquet like "Duke City." Pie Town is for real.

I've never gone to the real Pie Town because until now I've never had a tour guide. This day I've got one of the best imaginable: eighty-year-old Edd Jones, a battered little gent who used to make the pies that made Pie Town famous.

I met Jones at Datil, twenty-four miles to the east. It didn't take much—he turned down a free cup of coffee, in fact, to get him to join me on a trip to his former residence. In return for a ride to Pie Town, Jones would introduce me to old friends and to a place that lives in the heart—and stomach—of anyone who appreciates nostalgia.

These days, Edd ("Don't fergit the second *d*") Jones rarely gets back to Pie Town. He lives in Datil alone, save for a mutt named Midget, in a dilapidated, one-room cabin that sits next to an abandoned boxcar. This has not been a good winter for Jones, a lifelong bachelor. Fever blisters dot his homely face. The 7,500-foot elevation of this part of Catron County hasn't helped him. To battle recurring flu and breathing problems, he keeps a respirator in his tiny house. Through the goodness of the people who run Datil's Eagle Guest Ranch, Jones is provided room and board. Stooped and hobbled by a bum leg, Jones no longer cooks. But he is strong enough to go home to Pie Town.

Several stories exist as to how Pie Town acquired its name. The most commonly accepted concerns a man named Clyde Norman. After service in World War I, Norman came to western Catron County, homesteaded in a mud and log shack, then started serving coffee and pie to the cowboys and sheepherders who passed by. When it came time to name Norman's settlement, which stands halfway between Socorro and Springerville, Arizona, 175 miles from Albuquerque, the tag of Pie Town stuck. It has since become one of the most unusual and best-remembered place names in New Mexico or anywhere.

The promise of Pie Town spread quickly in the 1920s and 1930s. Dust bowl refugees showed up in droves. Most came from Texas and arrived penniless. All they owned they carted on the back of trucks. The juniper-and-piñon terrain may have come cheap, but it was no pie in the sky. Pie Town's short growing season made pinto bean farming, the chief source of income, an iffy proposition. Some Pie Town settlers stayed, but many left. In *No Life for a Lady*, Agnes Morley Cleaveland's 1941 classic of ranch life near Datil, the author writes of the Pie Town homesteader: "He walked, he grubbed, he starved. His bean crop failed far too frequently, his little patch of corn wilted with too great regularity under prolonged drought. Beaten, he moved on. . . ."

In its heyday, Pie Town had about 300 families. Now it has perhaps 100 residents. Most are poor and live simply. Pie Town has never been a la mode. Edd Jones arrived in Pie Town, or "this country," as he and just about everyone else who lives here calls the area, in 1932 from Snyder, Texas. His parents, who came with him, settled on a piece of land west of town. This being the depression and times being tough, Jones went to work in the town's cafe, the one that served the celebrated pies. For more than a decade he baked for governors and tourists and cowboys and anybody else who happened on to this country.

Hard of hearing and bashful, Jones says little as we drive to Pie Town. But when I ask him about pies, he doesn't stop talking. "We served them at fifteen cents a slice," Jones begins. He is wearing a stained ball cap, ski parka, and khaki trousers two sizes too big. "The cafe at first only had a wood stove. I learned to cook from my mother back in Texas when I was a boy. Just kinda picked up pies. My favorite? Coconut cream. Lots of people in this country liked that one." Jones says he baked an average of ten pies a day, fifteen on Sunday. Normally it took him twenty minutes to make one. Since every cook has his own way of doing things, Jones says it's bad to give advice. Tugging at the bill of his cap, he offers some tips anyhow:

Watch measurements. "If you're gonna make two pies, use a quarter cup of water. Making one, use half that."

Take care using milk. "If your milk boils over, you might just as well throw it out. Boiled milk takes all the sweetness out of a pie."

Make good crust. "No matter how much you fiddle, if the crust ain't good, the pie won't be."

Let the pie cool naturally. "Worst thing in the world is to put a pie in the refrigerator. Even settin' it on a windowsill ain't good."

For most travelers heading east or west on U.S. 60, Pie Town appears only as a gas station and general store on the north side of the highway. This is in fact New Pie Town. Old Pie Town, the place that grew up around the fabled cafe, lies to the south, a half-mile away on a side road. Ever since U.S. 60 was rerouted some years back, few tourists see Old Pie Town. It's the kind of place you don't go looking for unless you know it's there.

Climbing slowly out of the car, Jones gives me a tour of the old downtown. There was a time, he says, when the main street bustled and its buildings were bright. Pie being the all-American dish, many stores in town were painted red, white, and blue. Today, Pie Town is a drab gray ghost town.

Jones's health may be bad, but not his memory. This was the old post office, he says, pointing to a sagging shed; Arch McPaul was the postmaster. This is where J. V. Wyche had his taxidermy shop. And Aubrey Redwine his garage. Over there was Guy Melton's barbershop. The Pie Town Hotel, a sturdy log building, survives. It has, however, been decades since anyone but a vagrant slept in one of its three rooms. Peering into the hotel's doorway, Jones laughs so hard he begins coughing. "Ain't no Grand Central Hotel, is it?" he asks.

The shell of the general store remains. Harmon Craig was the first owner. Arriving in 1928 from Jacksboro, Texas, Craig picked up where Clyde Norman left off. Later, one J. A. Keele would run the community. But it was Craig, a red-haired prospector with a penchant for cussing, who struck it rich in Pie Town. He opened the hotel and some tourist cabins. And he pumped dough—both the green stuff and the floury kind—into the town's centerpiece, the cafe. Where the cafe once stood is now empty space. It seems strange to Jones that the hub of downtown has disappeared. On Saturday nights, people from all over this country would drive horse and buggy to Pie Town to eat. Jones would ride his quarter horse Snip to work at the rough-hewn but tidy little restaurant. "It had five tables," Jones recalls, glancing around at the barren ground. "Each sat four people. There were ten stools at the counter. We were open from 5:00 A.M. to midnight."

Jones not only cooked, but also helped Harmon Craig's wife can the vegetables and fruits she grew and served in the cafe. Pumpkin and cherry pies in Pie Town were home-grown. Despite his devotion to duty, Jones was paid only a dollar a day. "I'm ashamed to admit that," he says softly. "Course, I did get my meals." As Pie Town's top banana, Harmon Craig was careful with his money, though not too careful. "He didn't believe in banks," says Jones. "He'd hide the cafe money in a tote sack, then stick that under the sink in the wash room." Regardless of what he earned, for Jones the joys of short-order cooking were enough. He once witnessed a young man consume two coconut cream pies at a sitting. Rubbing his eyes, Jones says, "People always liked my pies."

Leaving the downtown area, Jones leads the way up a nearby street for a tour of various homes. The first house belongs to Beatrice Crawford, a grandmotherly woman with a generous smile. Crawford moved to Pie Town with her husband in 1937, from Abilene, Texas. She is delighted to see Jones, as is everyone he meets this day. There is something about Jones's innocence that warms people, that makes them forget their woes and encourages them to put out a welcome mat. Jones represents the past, a time when Pie Town prospered. And the past is always better than the present. Even before we sit down in the living room of her log home, a room which holds a large knick-knack collection, Crawford begins to lament the changes in Pie Town. There are no pie festivals any more. No bingo games, no community sings, no dances, no county fairs, no cowboy polo matches. The Baptist minister has even resigned. "Nothing happens here any more," Crawford reports. "Edd, you don't even make your cherry pie no more." Jones nods sympathetically. Even the town bar is gone, notes Crawford. It burned down in 1945. When questioned about what the bar was like, Crawford shakes her white-haired head. "Ask Edd," she says with a giggle, "he ought to know." "Frank Wilson owned it and was bartender," reveals Jones eagerly. "Gus Raney was the deputy sheriff here then. Gus was the law in Pie Town. All he had to do was look at a drunk and the guy'd fall down."

Catty-corner from Beatrice Crawford's house is the small clapboard home of Jack Keele, son of the late J. A. Keele, once one of Pie Town's leading citizens. We catch Keele, a stockily built carpenter, just as he is leaving for work. Pausing to put an arm around Jones, Keele booms, "Edd was one of the best pie makers in this whole country."

Jack Keele was ten when his family came to Pie Town in 1933 from Dimmitt, Texas. His story is typical: "We loaded everything in a 1928 Chevy truck. When we got here, we had just six cents." For Jack Keele, the old cafe and Jones represent a period that is sorely missed. "The cafe had no menu. You went in and asked them what they had to eat. There was only one entree. Golly, I liked Edd's cream pies. That cafe was unique and different. In its later years it had a kerosene refrigerator. Once upon a time it had a hole in the wall with a screen wire over the back of it." Keele wonders if we are going to eat in Pie Town this day. Before we can answer, he says, "Well, you got only one place to go."

The original cafe, the one where Edd Jones toiled, closed in the early 1950s. World War II plus several bad years of bean farming had slowed business, and the cafe never recovered. It was torn down in the early 1970s. Ten years before, a new cafe opened on new U.S. 60, in New Pie Town. It's still the only place in the community to eat pies or anything else. The little restaurant is called Break 21, a term truck drivers use on CB radios.

Truckers are the most frequent customers at the Break 21, according to Lester Jackson. Jackson and his wife, Emily, bought the cafe in 1976. With tattoos covering his sinewy forearms, and his gray hair clipped short, Les Jackson looks like the ex-Marine he is. Before retiring to Pie Town, he says he put in four tours of duty in Vietnam. Jackson may be a newcomer to Pie Town, but he understands the place's history. He owns a special New Mexico license plate that reads PIETOWN. He lives in one of the oldest homes in the village, a log cabin he claims was built in 1913.

For the cook who helped to make Pie Town prominent, Jackson holds special affection. "You want a spoon or a straw with your soup, Edd?" asks Jackson of my toothless tour guide. Reticent Jones may be, but when he wants to he can zing one from the back burner: "Just keep your damn thumb out of the soup, Les."

The Break 21, like its predecessor, hasn't forgotten the value of the town's distinguished dish. After consuming unmemorable roast beef and mashed potatoes, I order for eighty-five cents a slice of apple pie Jackson made from scratch. The pie's crust is light, and I acknowledge that fact. Jones grins. That brings the talk around to pie ingredients. "You know how to make the crust real flaky?" Jackson asks Jones. "You put beer in it." Jones looks at me as if to say, "That's a secret I forgot to tell you about."

Apple is the biggest seller in Pie Town these days. When the Jacksons purchased the Break 21, they put a plate on the wall indicating how many pies they have made. From February 1, 1976 to February 1, 1982, the number was 17,718. "Let me tell you a story about ol' Edd here," says Jackson, leaning over the counter of the cafe. "Edd can make a pie you wouldn't be able to tell what it was. He did that once here. Came in a couple of years ago and baked a pie that maybe two persons out of twenty could identify. One guy said pumpkin, another said something else. You know what that pie was? It was a pinto bean pie."

Fay Ford lives next door to the Break 21 Cafe. A cheerful woman who is wearing a floral-patterned blouse, Ford came to Pie Town with her husband in 1930 from Vernon, Texas. Like many current Pie Town residents, Ford is elderly and lives alone. (Her husband died five years after she arrived.) Most of her days are spent indoors. She would like to get out more, she admits, but can find no reason. "What we got to do," she says, "is get Edd back here to cook us up a dinner. That would get me out."

The next familiar face Edd sees is that of Margery McKinley. In this country for sixty-three years, she has strong recollections of the cafe. "Oh, that place was so pleasant. I always liked to go there to eat because it took me out of the kitchen." After Jones left Pie Town to take cooking jobs in Datil and Quemado for a time, McKinely's mother, Daisy Magee, ran the cafe. McKinley, whose face is strong and remarkably unlined, has seen Pie Town grow and wither. "Can't keep young people in this country," says the woman who reared seven children here. She can pinpoint when Pie Town acquired electricity (1942) and when telephone service came to the isolated community (1962). "Remember the movie theater, Edd? Bill Perry ran the show in the community center. The movies must have been about 100 years old."

Jones very much wants to see Opal Magee, Pie Town's postmistress. Unfortunately, she is out of town this day. Her assistant, a friendly young woman named Mary Hudson, tells us she has lived in Pie Town since she was two months old, and that she was schooled at home from the fifth grade on. Pie Town lost its two-teacher school in 1958. Today, children are bused twenty-three miles west to Quemado. If one lives on a Pie Town ranch, as Mary Hudson did, transportation is still difficult. Hudson's husband, Melvin, drills oil wells and builds windmills. When the couple were first married, they lived in Roswell for two months. "That's all I could take," explains Hudson. "I told my husband I wanted to go home, to Pie Town."

There are forty-eight postal boxes in use at Pie Town, and about fifteen persons on the mail route. Hudson says people stop in at the post office nearly every day to ask for a souvenir postmark. Others simply want to mail letters from Pie Town. "Even now," says Hudson, "there's something fascinating about those pies Edd made."

Just east of the post office on U.S. 60 is New Pie Town's only store, Lehew's Grocery. On its front steps this afternoon is a three-legged dog. Inside, a heavyset woman named Judy Lehew greets us. Lehew's grocery used to sell post cards of Old Pie Town. Motorists periodically ask her about the community's origin. She has her own explanation. "The way I heard it was that some fellow was hauling dried fruit west when his truck broke down. After that happened, he started making dried-fruit pies, then sold them. Now nobody makes dried-fruit pies anymore. Not even Edd." Judy Lehew came to Pie Town in 1955. Her father-in-law, John Lehew, came to this country in 1921. "He'd like to see you, Edd, I'm sure," says Mrs. Lehew.

John Lehew's three-room log cabin is located seventeen, often impassably muddy miles north of Pie Town. As we drive over a quagmire-like road, Edd says, "John's about the toughest old guy in this country." Indeed, at age eighty-seven, Lehew still rides a horse every day, climbs windmills, chops wood, and butchers hogs. He is the last of the first group of Pie Town settlers, the ones who came before the depression.

Six decades eking out a living in Pie Town have knotted Lehew's hands like oak limbs. His skin is the shade of that tree's bark. On Lehew's head sits a hat that looks like a knapsack pulled inside out. It is only when he takes off the hat that the years peel away. Lehew has a full head of hair and not one strand is gray. "You get this way," he says, "by not minding other people's business. Right, Edd?"

Lehew has lived by himself in his original homesteader's cabin since December 19, 1976. That's when his wife, Oddie, died. A stiff neck prevents him from driving a car. The last time he went into town was ten months before. I ask if he ever gets lonely. "Well," he says, "I had some visitors last month. And ol' Edd's here now." Between guests, Lehew spends time listening to the radio. Toward dusk, he moves over and switches on a television. He likes to watch professional wrestling.

John Lehew made his money running cattle. He bought out other homesteaders and saved. "Squeezed the eagle," he says. Hanging on his kitchen wall is an example of how he survived when other early Pie Towners quit. It's a Remington .22 automatic Lehew ordered from Sears when he first came to New Mexico. He purchased a thousand rounds of ammunition. "People thought I was crazy. But then I killed enough jackrabbits—sold their pelts for ten cents or fifteen cents—to pay for the rifle."

From Lehew's place, we backtrack toward Pie Town to see the Norris brothers. Granville Norris, seventy-three, lives on the land his father, Sam, settled in 1935. Granny's younger brother, Rex, resides a couple of miles away. The Norris brothers are like many long-time Pie Towners: they seem grim from years of hard work, until they spot their old pal, Edd Jones. "I ain't gonna say too much bad about Edd because he's got a stick there," Rex Norris says, pointing to the cane in Jones's hand. "I'll tell you what, though. There's still no better cafe cook in this country." Granny Norris nods in agreement. "We sure ate some good meals there, Edd. I reckon you made enough pies to stretch from here to New York." "Had some pretty good times at the cafe, too," adds brother Rex. "Edd, remember when somebody sprinkled black pepper all over the top of your stove?"

"It was red pepper," corrects Edd, chuckling. "And I still think you done it, Rex."

"Well, Edd," continues Rex, "I haven't forgotten the night I stayed in the Pie Town Hotel and found a big old boulder in my bed. You did that, didn't you?"

The Norris boys originally came to Pie Town because a third brother, Jimmy, suffered from asthma. "Soon as we landed in this country," explains Rex, "Jimmy got better. If you look at Jimmy today [he lives in Socorro], you wouldn't think he was ever sick. You can't beat the air and the elbow room here." Sam Norris and his wife were good friends with Edd's parents, J. A. and Mary Jones. In homesteading days, nearly everyone in Pie Town was close. The Norrises and Edd's folks are buried side by side in the Pie Town cemetery. Edd says he'll be laid to rest there, too.

As the Norris brothers say goodbye, they can't resist ribbing Jones about never marrying. Rex tells Jones he still has a chance: "Lots of widows would like your pies, Edd." A sudden fit of laughter and coughing convulses Jones. Lowering his voice, Rex Norris says knowingly, "You just got to love old Edd, don't you?"

Leaving Pie Town with a tuckered-out Edd Jones alongside me, I think about Rex Norris's comment. Not one person in town was less than pleased to see Jones. And friendly conversation was all Jones had to offer. Jones never has had any money. Even half-well he is one of the most forlorn-looking souls in this country. But "you've just got to love old Edd." Why? He is good, and so was Pie Town's past. Goodness is probably Jones's best secret of all, and that's what people remember most—that and his cooking.

Main Street

"Care for a cigar?"

I'm standing in the center of Glenrio, a deserted town that hugs the Texas border as a scared child does its mother. While a wicked winter wind slashes through my parka—this is the kind of New Mexico weather when you need to carry rocks in your pockets—I'm standing here, looking for U.S. Highway 66. Actually, the aged roadway lies beneath me. It's a buckled and weed-dressed macadam strip that dead-ends twenty-five yards away.

The idea was this: I'd go from one side of New Mexico to the other—Texas to Arizona—in search of a trail that was once America's Main Street. I'd be like Tod or Buzz, those footloose guys on the old "Route 66" television show. They got their kicks every week on 66, you'll recall, in a snappy Corvette convertible.

So here I am in a dented Jeep Cherokee with a bad accelerator. And what do I get for kicks? Ten-cent cigars. Homer Ehresman is offering the smokes. A flinty soul in soot-black sunglasses, Homer is about all there is to Glenrio, the farthest point east in New Mexico on old U.S. 66. Homer isn't offended that I turn down the cigars. Somebody sent them to him with a note of thanks, but he doesn't know who. "When 66 went through here," Homer says, rubbing his jaw, "lots of people needed help. This was a 'helper' town, like many on

66 was. In helper towns, you took care of people in bad weather or ones whose axle broke. Nobody needs help here now. Nobody stops here anymore 'less they're lost."

Homer stopped for good in Glenrio in 1935 when 66 was a dirt road. He ran a cafe and dispensed a teaspoon of nutmeg to travelers who couldn't tolerate the water. Homer hasn't soothed an upset stomach since way before Interstate 40 was put in nearly a dozen years ago. He doesn't mind. He even jokes about living in a forgotten place. The biggest joke, says Homer, is that if you want to get to Glenrio from New Mexico now, you have to go to Texas first, then circle back. Honest. The new expressway may be fancy, says Homer, but nobody who built it knew how to set up exits.

After bidding Homer good-day, I go back into Texas to return to New Mexico. In lots of places I-40 still gets called U.S. 66. But not by me. I know there is an old road out there that's not part of the interstate system at all. My idea then is twofold: I will hunt the old highway, and I will travel it whenever I can. At times, that will be easy, for in some stretches of New Mexico, U.S. 66 remains the main drag or at least a frontage road. Other times it will be difficult. In many spots across the state, the two-lane blacktop that ran from Chicago to Los Angeles has been buried beneath freeway concrete. In still other places, U.S. 66's bleached-out yellow stripe terminates at some lonely barricade.

After leaving Homer and his cigars, I find 66 again near Endee. Funny thing about Endee. Thanks to I-40, Endee has been moved three times. Once Endee was relocated from Glenrio, but that's another story. Suffice it to say that if you've seen Endee, which takes approximately six seconds of my time, you can travel the old highway all the way to San Jon. Until the summer of 1981, I-40 joined 66 to run clean through San Jon. Finally, the town was bypassed, one of the last holdouts in New Mexico to be amputated from the big highway. I find indications that the surgery has finished off San Jon. Motels and trinket shops display CLOSED signs. Once San Jon was a notorious speed trap. Now traffic along 66 moves too slowly. All of this has made for an awful lot of angry people in town.

Because I want to talk with a happy person, I go see Clark White. A prudent man with merry blue eyes and snowy hair, White was born in San Jon in 1908. For many years he operated a Conoco station on 66. He remembers the highway when *Grapes of Wrath* Okies rattled through San Jon in flatbed trucks groaning with a lifetime's worth of possessions. Years later, Sammy Davis, Jr., pulled into White's gas station in a purple Eldorado.

Clark White deals with the realities of a highway bypass by recalling the good times the old trail gave him. In his garage he shows me a 1922 Model T roadster that he maintains and often takes for spins down what is left of 66. He asks me if I have heard the story about the two politicians who years ago got stuck on 66. I tell him I haven't. "Well, one fella's car was headed west, the other fella's car was headed east, when each of them hit the mud. Neither car could go forward. They didn't know what to do. Finally, the men swapped cars and, like a lot of politicians will do, they backed out."

From a desk in his living room, White removes a dogeared document. His eyes brighten at the sight of a 1917 *Texas–New Mexico Log Book*. Before 66 received its name in 1937, it was known by lots of titles. Once it was Road 6 in parts of the state. Once it was Road 3. A long time ago, it was the Ozark Trail. Then the Will Rogers Highway. Far, far back, when it went from Amarillo, Texas, to Las Vegas, New Mexico, the road was called the Texas–New Mexico Highway.

White's log book contains no map. Tourists in the Southwest didn't use maps in those days, according to White. They went by a list of directives: "sound your horn," "jog left," "ravine ahead," "follow winding road." "That was a time," says White, "when you had to get out and open and close ranch gates." Putting away the log book, White gets a faraway look in his eyes. "I raised two kids right on Highway 66 in a house next to my gas station. It probably wasn't the best place to raise kids, but things turned out all right. The highway gave me a living. But nothing lasts forever."

After explaining to me that I can follow old 66 all the way to Tucumcari, White tells me something else. "Stay out of the mud," he cautions.

Tucumcari is also a recent bypass victim. Motel customers here were once lulled to sleep by trucks downshifting through town. My motel, which advertises Longboy beds, is silent as a sepulcher. Still, a mileage indicator at the motel's front desk reveals the best way to reach California: Highway 66. A neon marker on the roof of the motel proclaims the inn to be American-owned and -operated. Many of Tucumcari's old 66 hostelries, I learn, are now run by Pakistanis and East Africans. "They're not very friendly," a longtime Tucumcari resident says of the foreign entrepreneurs in town. "They're all business.

If they think you swiped a washcloth from your room, they're liable to chase you down the highway to get it."

Years ago, gangsters John Dillinger and Pretty Boy Floyd slipped into Tucumcari on 66 and bedded down at Hampton's Tourist Courts, now the Third Street Grocery. The next morning the outlaws ate at the Waffle House, now a dress shop. I learn all this from Ray Paulson, an amiable, pear-shaped fellow who has lived in Tucumcari since depression days. Paulson asks me if I have ever heard of Metropolitan Park. I shake my head. Motioning for me to follow, he drives four miles west of town on old 66. We arrive at a shady grove and a huge hole in the ground. This, Paulson claims, pointing to the hole, is the biggest swimming pool in New Mexico.

Ray Paulson came from Wisconsin to run the Metropolitan Park pool. He held that job for thirty-five years. Paulson is large, but the pool is larger. Shaped like a giant footprint, the pool is 180 feet long and 100 feet wide. It can hold 400,000 gallons of water. Once it held 500 bathers. "If you motored through and stayed in Tucumcari on 66," says Paulson, lowering his bulk down a ladder onto the empty pool's twelve-foot-deep bottom, "there was a good chance you swam here. See, our summers are scorchers. I had grown people come by and tell me their parents took them in here when they were kids crossing the country." Young men from the Civilian Conservation Corps built the pool. The flagstones for the deck and the pine railings for the bath house were hauled in from nearby Mesa Redondo. More than 100 Chinese elms were taken from the edge of 66 and transplanted around the park's grounds. The project was completed in 1938.

"Nobody ever drowned on me," says Paulson, pacing off the floor of the pool. "I know where every line and pipe and drain in this place is. I kept the water at seventy-eight degrees. I put. . . ." I interrupt Paulson to ask why the pool has no water. He explains that the city of Tucumcari shut down Metropolitan Park four years ago when the city opened a normal-size swimming pool in the middle of town. The new pool is named for a businessman who, it happens, left this world in a U.S. 66 auto accident. "It was all a political thing," says Paulson of the closing. "There was no other reason. And it's a damn shame. This pool doesn't leak; it's solid. I could have it working in two days. Let me show you the filter system. . . ."

Heading west from Tucumcari, I can still find pieces of 66 at wide spots in the road like Montoya, Newkirk, and Cuervo. You can get gasoline in Cuervo if you don't mind waiting for the attendant to put his toothpick on top of the cash register, a routine that can take as long as five minutes. According to State Highway Department records, in 1923 an estimated ninety-three vehicles went by these little towns every twenty-four hours. Because the villages now sit beside the big interstate, the figure is up to 9,000 cars every day.

By the time I reach Santa Rosa I am ready for lunch. Years ago, 66 used to wind its way from Santa Rosa to Albuquerque by taking a peculiar detour to Santa Fe. That route was changed—and straightened—when someone apparently realized that the shortest distance between the two points was not a semicircular path past the state capital.

At Truckstops of America, on the east end of Santa Rosa, I ease myself into a booth across from a thin-faced man with a creased brow. John Seay is coating a T-bone steak in A.1. sauce. I tell him to go ahead and eat, we can talk later. When he's finished, Seay wipes his mouth and tells me in a smoky Southern drawl that he is sixty-two years old, from Scottsville, Virginia, and that he has been a truck driver for forty years. I ask him to tell me what driving 66 was like.

"Way, way back it was a tricky road. It was always shifting. You could go for miles and miles and wouldn't hit a bump. It was kind of narrow, sure. And some of them hills was treacherous. You had to be careful about filling stations. There weren't that many and a fella who ran one might close down and go to Florida for the winter and you'd be stuck. But no question, 66 was the superhighway of its day."

Seay says that when he drove 66 he never made a beeline through the countryside, like he does today on the bland, fenced-in interstate. A trip through New Mexico was an adventure. He'd stop to gather lava rocks for his kids. He'd pull over and feed soybeans to prairie dogs. He'd get out of his truck to help an Indian boy fly a kite. He'd hunt for bottles. On the outskirts of Albuquerque, Seay once found a six-ounce Coca-Cola bottle. "Still got it; worth about thirty-five dollars now."

While a waitress refills his water glass, Seay tells me that everything on 66 was "last chance." Last chance to gas up before the mountains. Last chance to eat before the desert. If you didn't see a last-chance sign, says Seay, you saw one advertising Burma Shave. (Those are now collectors' items, like his Coke bottle.)

Even before CB radios came along, places had code names among truckers, says Seay. Tucumcari was "the Gorge." Arizona was "the Desert." Seay drove 66 when rattlesnakes would find their way into a truck's cargo. He drove it when a trucker placed a sheet of plastic over the water bag he carried on his radiator. The plastic was to keep the raccoons off the bag at night. A comforting recollection stays with Seay. "Used to be a fella around here called himself Parson Brown. He'd ride old 66 on a mule. Parson Brown, he preached to anybody. And he prayed for all the truckers."

A truck loaded with toxic and foul-smelling chemical pesticides once caught fire along Interstate 40. When the fire was extinguished, the owners of the truck suggested that instead of hauling it off to a waste dump, the truck be buried where it stood, in Clines Corners. Like a secondhand rug, Clines Corners has a way of being stepped on constantly. If the "Tonight Show" originated from New Mexico, Johnny Carson would know where to aim his waggish buckshot: at Clines Corners. On my car radio I find that an Albuquerque radio station has already targeted Clines Corners. The station, nearly every half-hour since I left Glenrio, has been promoting a wine sold in pop-top cans. The wine, disk jockeys swear, with tongues firmly in cheeks, is fermented in "beautiful downtown Clines Corners."

Perhaps the granddaddy of all New Mexico souvenir emporiums, Clines Corners has a rich history. Roy E. Cline, a New Mexico homesteader, bought the property from the state in 1935. Cline convinced the Continental Oil Company to have his purchase, fifty-eight miles east of Albuquerque, put on all Rand McNally road maps. Cline sold gas and other products. He then left in 1938, apparently taking his apostrophe with him. Today, Clines Corners is one of I-40's most recognizable tourist centers, a 139-acre compound of ten buildings, nine mobile homes, and twenty-eight gasoline pumps. There is a post office (ZIP code 87070), a 140-seat cafeteria (twenty-nine-cent coffee) and eighty employees, most of whom compose what is known as the unincorporated village of Clines Corners.

If Clines Corners bustles—the cafeteria serves on the average 1,000 meals a day—why then is it so often the subject of cruel jabs? (Clines Corners is so ugly, goes one joke, that its chickens wear bags over their heads.) There are several reasons for the ridicule. Bad weather is one. Clines Corners is not a good place to be caught in a snowstorm, as many travelers often are. It can be wind-swept and bitterly cold. And during the heat of summer, pesky June bugs have been known to march into Clines Corners like the Prussian Army. The food at Clines Corners has never received rave reviews, either. The hamburger I order seems to be missing something. A middle-aged diner in a green jumpsuit appears to know what it is. From a nearby table he hands me a large bottle of Tabasco sauce.

But it is the "rubber tomahawk trade" that draws most visitors, and laughs, to Clines Corners. In the gift shop, the smell of cedar piggy banks nearly knocks me over. Indian doodads are the hottest items, and it doesn't matter which Indians made them or where those Indians dwell. I spot moccasins manufactured in Minnesota, head-dresses stitched in North Carolina, gourd rattles from Haiti, and "ancient Indian pottery," depicting buttes and mesas, handcrafted in butte-scattered Wisconsin. The manager-owner of Clines Corners Operating Company has a sense of humor, thank goodness. After ordering plastic tom-toms for thirteen years, Doug Murphy says he has learned to laugh at the jokes and even crack a few of his own. When a military helicopter touched down briefly in front of Clines Corners and a tourist asked Murphy what it was all about, Murphy replied, straight-faced, that the chopper belonged to the Clines Corners Air Force.

Ten miles east of Moriarty, I decide to see what is happening at the Longhorn Ranch, another tourist spot I had observed for several years. Conceived by an ex-highway patrolman in the late 1930s, the Longhorn Ranch for nearly three decades was one of 66's chief road-side attractions. A re-created western village, the ranch featured a restaurant, saloon, bank, feed store, and museums. Totem poles welcomed travelers; stagecoach and pony rides were available. In the back, a live bear on a chain once waved its paws.

In pre-interstate days, the Longhorn did a half million dollars worth of business a year. Along about 1960, however, the place became the quintessential white elephant. Repeatedly it was sold or auctioned. In 1972, two businessmen from New York City were the buyers. The pair announced grandiose plans to return the Longhorn to prominence. Within months the men had sold the contents of the museum, which included antique automobiles, priceless clocks, and a circa-1880 bar top. The New Yorkers left the ranch in the lurch.

Earlier this year, a mammoth, jolly Floridian named Wayne Hayes purchased the Longhorn from a San Diego, California, bank. I ask Hayes how much he paid for the place. "I ain't gonna tell ya," he replies with a wink. "But I will say this. I stole the dang thing."

Hayes plans to open the restaurant soon and to restore what else is restorable. "Them last owners," he says, "they stripped her clean. The rest's been vandalized bad. Heck, we had to tear down fourteen buildings." Hayes confesses he bought the Longhorn mainly for its acreage. Hayes is a horse trainer. He will use the back pasture, out where people gawked at the tethered bear, to raise thoroughbreds. I wish him good luck. "We're not going to need much luck," Hayes says, winking.

It is still possible to journey from Moriarty to Albuquerque on old 66. It's a teeter-totter ride around mountain towns, past ghostly eateries, and finally through Dead Man's Curve in Tijeras Canyon, which has ghosts of its own.

In Albuquerque, 66 becomes a boulevard of neon known as Central Avenue. Residents of New Mexico's largest city tell me that on occasion they have glimpsed, poking out from behind a telephone pole on Central, an old 66 sign. Its once-familiar white shield design and black numbers have caused some to stop and look again. I look for these signs but find none. When I inquire at the State Highway Department office, I am told all 66 markers have been removed, scraped, repainted, and placed on other highways. But aren't they in demand? I ask Bob Ringer, head of the department's traffic safety division. "Sure," he says. "It's nostalgic. It's a romantic part of America that has been lost forever." Do you have any of those signs left, I press, trying to imagine how one would look on my den wall. "One," replies Ringer. "Only it looks as if someone used it for bayonet practice."

Jack Rittenhouse owns no U.S. 66 signs. But if there is one person in Albuquerque who can tell a tale or two about the highway, it is he. A lumpy-looking gent with a whisk-broom mustache, Rittenhouse lives just six blocks south of old 66. For most of his working life Rittenhouse edited, published, or collected books on the Southwest. Once upon a time he was a young Los Angeles, California, advertising copywriter who hoped to write a book. Like all advertising types, Rittenhouse had an idea. His was to put together a travel guide to Highway 66. The year was 1946. With World War II and gasoline rationing over, Rittenhouse knew Americans would be climbing on 66 like moths on a night light.

The only way to do a guidebook, Rittenhouse explains, is to view a subject firsthand. "I took off from L.A. in the spring. Drove by myself in a 1939 American Bantam. You probably haven't heard of that car; few people have. It was kind of like the Jeep you're driving, only the American Bantam had no power to go up hills. The nice thing about it was that it got fifty-five miles to the gallon."

Averaging only thirty miles an hour, Rittenhouse guided his Bantam through Needles, California; Kingman, Arizona; Oklahoma City, Oklahoma; Joplin, Missouri; and on into Chicago. It took him a month. In his left hand he held the steering wheel. With his right hand he made notes on a scratch pad. Intermittently, he'd check his dashboard altimeter. "People back then," he says, "wanted to know all about the grade of the highway." Each evening Rittenhouse would stop in a motor court and type up his notes. When he reached Chicago, he doubled back to check his facts—spellings of lodgings and cafes, distances, and descriptions of historic sites.

The guidebook appeared in late 1946 and sold for one dollar. The book was pocket-size and 130 pages in length. Its purpose was to prepare travelers for the excitement of the open road, not for a rubbernecking joyride. Rittenhouse did this by offering such tips as, "It's not a bad idea to carry one of those war-surplus foxhole shovels." Certain items Rittenhouse purposely left out of his book. Such as the shop in Grants that took cockleburs, soaked them in white paint, and then passed them off to sightseers as porcupine eggs. Or the Santa Rosa tourist cabins' owner who painted his cement floors dark blue so as to resemble plush carpeting. Or the long-gone hotel in Continental Divide that was more than likely a combination rest stop and bordello.

Rittenhouse drew all the maps, and printed and marketed the text himself. He sold 3,000 copies. "It's a rare book now," says the author, handing over a copy and telling me to keep it. Feeling almost as if I am receiving the Gutenberg Bible, I don't know what to say. Rittenhouse speaks for me. "No one," he says, "is ever going to write another one of these."

A half-century ago, 66 left Albuquerque and went south through the Isleta Indian Reservation to Peralta, then across the Rio Grande to Los Lunas. From there the road headed northwest till it reached the Rio Puerco. Most travelers, however, remember 66 as the highway that chugged in and out of Albuquerque via Nine Mile Hill, a long incline on the western end of the city.

Near the crest of Nine Mile Hill, out past where the 66 Drive-in once stood, an X-rated movie theater that irate citizens turned into a park, Esteban Herrera lives in his dream house. Herrera, bowlegged and seventy-nine, speaks little English. His face bears the pleats of someone who has spent years on the range. Indeed, for most of his life Herrera has worked ranches in the Rio Puerco and Cañoncito areas, along 66. After decades of saving, Herrera in the early 1970s bought five acres of the old Atrisco Land Grant. In 1976, after still more scrimping, he completed a mini-Taj Mahal on the property.

I had seen Herrera's imposing estate from the interstate before and had always been curious about its eerie isolation: no neighbors for miles, a 100-yard-long driveway. Who could live there? On this trip I stop to find out. Herrera is happy to show me around his big, white two-story home. On our way up the long drive, he tells me that dream houses don't come cheap: the fence that surrounds his land cost $7,000. The remote-controlled gate cost $1,600. A well out back ran $23,000.

Herrera's living room is without furniture, and I never learn why. Because Herrera eats most of his meals in restaurants on Central Avenue, the kitchen is bare, too. On the second floor, which is reached by a spiral staircase, is Herrera's bedroom. A large, new telescope sits in one corner. It is pointed not at a window, but at a wall. Herrera says the telescope's instruction manual warns gazers that they can go blind by looking at the sun.

With great pride Herrera shows me a sundeck off the bedroom. The view of the Sandia Mountains is magnificent and unobstructed. I find it hard, however, to visualize this old cowboy stripping down and oiling up with cocoa butter. I also have trouble trying to figure out where he would sit: the sundeck, too, is unappointed. A lifelong bachelor, Herrera will be the home's only occupant. His mother, Francisquitta, died shortly before her son completed the structure. I ask him if he gets lonely and Herrera shakes his head. When you live in a dream house, he says, there are always things to do.

From Nine Mile Hill, twenty-five miles rush by before I pick up 66 again. Snaking my way through Old Laguna and then New Laguna, I finally arrive at the crossroads of San Fidel. Greeting me inside that hamlet's only store is its vivacious owner, Mary Ann Tafoya. This day Tafoya is at work on reunion plans for St. Joseph's, the area's grammar school and proudest possession. She is writing to all the nuns who have ever taught at the institution and who are still living. Putting down her pen, Tafoya says the interstate bypassed San Fidel nearly fifteen years ago, but that tourists continue to wander into her Indian trading post. And with a boisterous laugh, she reports that yes, tourists continue to ask dumb questions. "We had one woman who came in here not long ago. She had seen some cows out near the highway and she asked us to call the zoo. She was worried the animals were loose."

Pushing back her long dark hair, Tafoya gives me more: "People want to know if I take American money. They want to know if they need a visa to get back to California. They ask where do we get our water and if we grow our own food."

For many years the Acoma Indians who hang about San Fidel obliged those excursionists arriving with inane inquiries. When the highway changed, so did the Indians. "Anybody who wants to photograph an Indian now," says Tafoya, "has to pay them a dollar."

If you lived in Grants during the 1950s, and you spoke in favor of a highway bypass, it was said you didn't have long to live. Despite years of bitter opposition, Grants was eventually circumvented. And strangely, the community survived quite well. Few residents now seem to mind the interstate that runs south of the city. Some persons in Grants even like I-40.

Take Walter and Dorothy McBride, for instance. Their home, just east of Grants, is located a good half-mile from old 66, but only twenty yards from the busy westbound lane of the interstate. The McBrides' estate is a massive, out-of-place-looking structure, odder in appearance than even Esteban Herrera's digs. The McBrides' highway hacienda has balconies and towers. With its vast red-tiled roof and the 22,000 tan bricks in its walls, the dwelling is more of a fortress than a family home. Indeed, some of the McBrides's neighbors call the 6,000-square-foot house a sand castle.

The McBrides moved in in 1977. A Grants contractor, Walter did a bang-up job on the interior. There are spiral staircases, twenty-two-foot vaulted ceilings, and a fireplace nearly large enough to heat the Astrodome. Unlike Esteban Herrera's home, the McBride place has almost too many chairs. Guiding me to a hassock, Dorothy McBride, an attractive, fashion-conscious young woman, pulls up a banquette. She says that she and her husband were reared in the Grants area. Walter grew up on U.S. 66 alongside his grandparents' landmark business, the Valencia Grocery, now a motorcycle shop. Dorothy says when she and her husband wed, they moved into an apartment in downtown Grants near another section of 66. "It was too noisy there," she recalls, "so we came out here by the interstate. We wanted a quiet place in the country."

When the interstate began unrolling itself across New Mexico in the 1950s, nobody said it would go down smoothly. The hardest task of all for the Highway Department was telling people their businesses or homes were blocking the new route. Most folks quietly gave in. One couple who did not were P. J. and Virginia Andreasen. Their little adobe stood twenty-five miles east of Gallup in the tiny village of Coolidge. When surveyors reached Coolidge, the Andreasens were told their front door opened on Interstate 40's median.

For six years the Andreasens refused to budge. Meanwhile, concrete was poured around them. Finally, in 1958, the New Mexico Highway Department gave the Andreasens an ultimatum: leave your house or go to jail. The embittered couple left, but not without a stinging farewell. They took a copy of the Constitution of the United States, placed it in a small coffin, draped the casket with an American flag, and paraded about New Mexico in protest.

Having heard of the Andreasens' ordeal, I put them on my itinerary. They still reside in Coolidge. Their new home is easy to spot; an American flag on a tall pole flies outside day and night. Mrs. Andreasen, fatigued-looking, in her late sixties, and wearing an expression of grave suspicion, talks to me from behind a padlocked gate. She cannot come out any farther, she says, because her husband is ill. I ask her about the American flag that people in Coolidge say never comes down. "We fly it because we're Americans," she snaps. "The state of New Mexico treated us like Russians."

P. J. Andreasen, his wife says, once worked for the Gideon Society of New Mexico. He put Bibles in motel rooms all along 66. Both Andreasens are Christian missionaries. They felt the devil did them in back in the 1950s. "The state took an acre of our land," says Mrs. Andreasen. "Two hundred beautiful piñon trees in all." I ask her why the $10,000 New Mexico finally paid her wasn't enough. She says that by the time she and her husband received the settlement, their fight had driven them deep into debt. "After we left our home, which we were ordered to tear down ourselves, by the way, we had to live in a tent. We had to cook our meals outside. Our lawyers were no help; they were in cahoots with the Highway Department. How can I still be mad? Look, how would you like it if someone took something of yours and gave you nothing in return?"

I depart Coolidge with a sour taste in my mouth. I feel sorry for the Andreasens, yet I remember what Clark White had said back in San Jon: it's no use crying about progress. In Gallup, I decide to look for someone with warmer memories of 66. I find them in Pauline Middleton, a tall, hospitable, gray-haired schoolteacher.

As we sit on the front steps of Roosevelt Elementary School, just south of where 66 forms Gallup's main thoroughfare, Middleton tells me she grew up on 66 in a home attached to what may have been the first motel in New Mexico. It was situated on the west edge of Gallup and bore the quaint name of Maggie & Jiggs Court. Built in the 1920s, the motel was initially nothing more than a campground. When twenty primitive cabins were erected, each was given a name from a comic strip: "Mutt and Jeff," "Skeezix," "Tillie the Toiler," "Andy Blossom."

Middleton's father bought the motel in 1927. She can remember helping him push a wheelbarrow loaded with stove wood around to the cabins. Lots of friendly people stayed in those cabins, including an official from the University of Minnesota who later gave Pauline a job when she went off to college there. For many years the Maggie & Jiggs's little white-with-green-trim cabins cost four dollars a night. Middleton says people traveled with their own linen and kitchen utensils in the early days of U.S. 66. When the cabins began to deteriorate, they were rebuilt and renamed the West Side Auto Court. In 1956, Middleton's parents sold out, and a few years after that the whole place was torn down. Today, the Golden Lion Cafeteria occupies the land. Nostalgia aside, life in a motor court had its good and bad aspects. "My parents got the bad," says Middleton. "They never could take a vacation together. I got the good: my parents were always home."

Twenty-odd miles from where Gallup's Maggie & Jiggs Court stood, U.S. 66 in New Mexico completes its course. To see exactly where the old route finishes, I follow it past rusted Meteor Crater signs, and bacon-tinted mesas, until I come to Fort Yellowhorse. Painted a garish lemon color, Fort Yellowhorse is a tourist trap gone to seed. The mock military post now huddles in a field of crabgrass. The only soldier about is an abandoned Buick. Nearby is a peculiar-looking rock formation billed as a cliff dwelling. At the foot of the alleged ruins is an Indian wishing well. "Always drop silver wampum," a placard urges.

Inside the fort's gift shop I meet the new manager, Mary Smith. John Yellowhorse, the attraction's original owner, appears to have seen the future of U.S. 66. Yellowhorse, Smith tells me, has become a full-time attorney on the Navajo Reservation. I ask the manager, an enthusiastic young Navajo, how things are going. Business is slow, she says, except for tobacco sales. The troops who stop at Fort Yellowhorse these days generally want only the reduced-price cigarettes, not a tour of the cliff dwelling. One side of the shop is marked "New

Mexico." The other side is designated "Arizona." "Better to buy cigarettes on Arizona side," says Smith with a smile. "Reason is taxes."

Back at my starting point of Glenrio, 370 miles to the east on 66, I had been offered a cigar. At Fort Yellowhorse, the end of the line, I am solicited with cigarettes. I figure there must be something symbolic to that (ashes to ashes?) but can't be sure just what it is. I am sure of something else, however. Sixty-six may have harbored traffic bottlenecks and radar nets. It may have specialized in cardboard cacti and bows and arrows made in Massachusetts. Its inns may have promised steam heat and screened porches. But even knowing all that, I determine this: given the chance to pass through life a second time, following a yellow stripe west would be a nice way to go.

In early 1985, the American Association of State Highway and Transportation Officials decertified U.S. 66. The move, in effect, wiped away the highway forever. A few months later, some Route 66 signs sold at auction for $370 each.

Los Arabes

You are the bows from which your children as
living arrows are sent forth.

Kahlil Gibran

Mystical poet Kahlil Gibran came to the United States from his native Lebanon in 1910. Though Gibran never reached the Southwest, his words were prophetic for those who did: in the last 100 years, Gibran's countrymen, like arrows, have left a mark on New Mexico.

No one is sure how many Lebanese have immigrated to New Mexico. A reasonable guess is that there are 1,500 people of Lebanese extraction living in the state, the second-largest foreign-born minority next to Italians.

First, some geography. A narrow stretch of earth about the size of Connecticut, Lebanon is situated at the eastern end of the Mediterranean Sea. Primarily an agricultural land, it has no oil. Of its estimated 2.6 million population in 1985, about half is Christian, the rest mostly Moslem. Arabic is the official language. Lebanon is believed to have been founded 4,000 years ago by the Phoenicians, who were great seafaring traders. It is a nation rich in biblical history: Jonah was supposedly cast upon the shoreline twenty miles south of Beirut, its largest city. Jesus is said to have walked the green hills. In more modern times, Lebanon has been, at various periods, under Turkish, Syrian, or French rule. Though independent since 1941, for many years Lebanon has been caught in the middle of the Arab-Israeli

dispute. For the last several years it has been rocked by gunfire, bomb-
ings, hostage crises, and assorted acts of terrorism.

It is often said that there are more Lebanese living outside the
country than within. The major exodus occurred in the late nine-
teenth and early twentieth centuries. Freedom of religion and a desire
to better oneself were chief reasons for leaving. But why go to New
Mexico? It was a frontier, a territory ripe with opportunity.

Though Lebanon has a much milder climate, the northern New
Mexico villages where most Lebanese settled were reminders of home.
It was from these communities that *los Arabes*, as they were called
by Hispanics, peddled wares as their Phoenician forefathers had done.
Certain Lebanese nomads figured to build a nest egg in New Mexico,
then return to the Old Country. A few did this, but many stayed,
giving New Mexico a people of great wit, love of family, and a willingness to work hard. *Los Arabes* who stayed on retained strong emotional ties with their homeland, bonds that survive today.

To discover what it means to be Lebanese in New Mexico, a good
person to start with is a balding, sixtyish man named Sam Adelo. An
erudite troubleshooter for Gulf Oil, Adelo is one of eight children
born to Assad Abdullah Abu Habib, in Pecos, about fifteen miles
southeast of the state capital.

From his comfortable office in Santa Fe, Adelo explains that his
late father, also called Sam Adelo, hailed, as do many Lebanese in
New Mexico, from Roumieh, an upland retreat ten miles from Beirut. And like many immigrants, the senior Adelo landed in Las Vegas,
New Mexico, in 1913. Aided there by Jewish wholesalers, Adelo sold
pots and pans out of a horse-drawn wagon. Eventually he relocated
to Pecos, where he set up a general store. The store, Adelo's, still
thrives, as does a second Pecos enterprise, Adelo's Town and Country Store. Both are run by Sam Junior's five brothers.

Sam Senior quickly became one of the best-known of *los Arabes*
in New Mexico: an honest and diligent merchant, a knowledgeable
politician, an American Army veteran of World War I. In Pecos, Sam
Senior broke tradition. His son explains: "Many Lebanese immigrants
of those days returned to the Old Country for a bride. My father was
different. He married a Hispanic."

Growing up half-Lebanese in Pecos was different, too, says Sam
the younger. Leaning back in his office chair, he recalls being cast as
a newsboy in a school play. Needing some newspapers for props, he
went home and grabbed copies of *Al-Hoda*, an Arabic-language pub-

lication his father subscribed to, a periodical a few older New Mexicans still take. When young Sam hawked the newspapers on stage, a howl was heard. "The people in the audience couldn't figure out what that crazy-looking newspaper was," Sam says. "They thought it was Chinese."

Though he has no children of his own, Sam Adelo believes few young Lebanese in New Mexico have an interest in their roots. "The farther away you get from the original immigrants, the more the customs die out. A lot of this is because young people don't get the chance to go to Lebanon." Because he works for an international company, Adelo has made many trips to the Middle East, and has been to Roumieh several times, though not in recent years. "The war over there makes it dangerous," he says. He keeps up with events through the American-Lebanese League, a heritage promotion group based in Washington, D.C. Adelo can't read Arabic, but he does speak some. To a visitor leaving his office, he offers, "Masalemeh"—"May God go with you."

An old proverb says this of the Lebanese businessman: "He can make a wine cellar out of a grape." The Lebanese community of New Mexico is filled with rags-to-riches stories. Two names stand out: Bellamah and Maloof.

Abdul Hamid Bellamah, better known as Dale, started out as a warehouse hand in Belen. Tenacity and foresight led Bellamah to strike it rich in the home-building business. His sprawling Princess Jeanne Park, in Albuquerque's Northeast Heights, was one of the city's first major housing developments. When Bellamah died in 1972, his personal wealth was estimated at between $30 million and $50 million.

George Maloof grew up in Las Vegas, where his father, Joseph, owned a general store. Young George helped the family acquire a statewide beer distributorship. Later, he added the First National Bank of Albuquerque, a trucking firm, hotels, and a professional basketball team, the Houston Rockets. When Maloof died in 1980, his empire had grown to a $125 million-a-year operation. Both men, like many other Lebanese entrepreneurs, were immensely philanthropic with their money.

Some say the work ethic among Lebanese originated with wives who pushed their husbands. Another Arab belief has it that if one labors hard, one will live long. Joseph Budagher, an Indian trader who set up shop near the Santo Domingo Pueblo, lived to ninety-four; Sam Adelo Sr., to eighty-eight. Yet modern-day pressures seem to work against this theory: Dale Bellamah and George Maloof died of heart attacks at fifty-seven.

For every enormously successful Lebanese businessman, like Albuquerque Realtor Joe Azar and the late Nathan Salmon, who made a fortune in Santa Fe movie theaters, there are others who have prospered on a smaller scale. Take for instance people like John Budagher, who with his brothers pilots a filling station–tavern–pool hall on Interstate 25, between Albuquerque and Santa Fe; or Shaheen and Jamiel Sawaya, who manage the Melmar Market in Raton; or Rose Malouf, who owns a maternity shop in Santa Fe; or the Tabet family, who have long been involved in real estate and law in Belen; or Pauline Hanosh Michael, proprietor of a dry-goods emporium and cafe in Cibola County's pin-dot-tiny town of Bibo.

In southeast Torrance County sits a faded little crossroads community called Duran. Once Duran was a bustling railroad division point, a homesteading hub of 2,500 residents. The arrival of the depression and the exit of a locomotive roundhouse reduced the population to seventy. And most of those are named Hindi.

Milhim (Bill) Hindi reached Las Vegas in 1908 from Zahle in the Lebanese plains. Bill's brother Alex joined him four years later. After Alex met a young girl named Clarita Duran, the brothers decided to settle in the town named after her family. There they opened a merchandise mart called Hindi Brothers, and in 1920, as their Bedouin ancestors had done, they began to raise sheep. The store has been closed since 1962, but the Hindi Sheep Company has expanded to a busy concern that sells about 2,500 animals every October. Alex and Bill Hindi have been dead for several years. The ranch today is owned by Alex's four cowboy-looking sons, Sam, Brahin, Nabay, and Shafei, all of whom live catty-corner from one another in downtown Duran.

In the beginning, Torrance County didn't know what to make of the Hindis, even though the Tabets and the Kouris, from Bhamdun, Lebanon, had been in and out of the area earlier. The name Hindi led many to believe the family was from India. Prejudice flared: Hindi boys were called "Turko" and "Gypsy," and fistfights resulted. The animosity ended when Sam Hindi and two of his brothers married local girls.

To gather the Hindi brothers together is to assemble curious bits of lore. Sam Hindi recalls that when one of his brothers would fall down, his father, a Moslem, would exclaim, "My Allah!"; Brahin has a recollection of his Uncle Bill smoking a water pipe called a *narghi-*

le, surely a strange sight for central New Mexico. Nabay, who visited Lebanon in 1949 with his parents, occasionally says "smolla" when someone sneezes.

That 1949 visit was a high point. The Hindis brought back several Arabian horses to breed and to enter in New Mexico's Pony Express Race held annually in Lincoln. The family usually does well in the event. The trip back home also afforded Nabay some insights into the differences between Lebanon and the Land of Enchantment. "The people over there seemed to enjoy living more than the people here," he says, walking toward a barn. At fifty-one, Nabay is the youngest of the brothers, yet he has a keen sense of historical perspective. He especially takes pleasure in analyzing the cultural obstacles his father faced. "When Dad first came to this country, he was very cautious, even on the defensive, as a lot of older Lebanese still are here. I can remember Dad used to say he was always thirsty at first. He was just shy to ask for a drink of water." Though Alex Hindi had only a third-grade education, he learned to speak and read in three languages. "Dad would listen to everyone—the president or a tramp," says Nabay, pausing by the barn door. "And he would study a person as he listened. He taught me to do that, too. I can kind of look at someone and after a while pretty much know what I want to know about that person. I guess you'd say that's a Lebanese way."

At one point, Albuquerque was home for two Lebanese restaurants. Now it has none. What it does have, however, are two outlets that specialize in Lebanese baked goods: Hakeem's and the Middle Eastern Bakery.

In the early days of statehood, all *los Arabes* in New Mexico would join forces once a year to eat and sing and reminisce. World War II ended that, and for the next twenty-five years or so the only time kinfolk gathered would be for weddings or funerals. Then, a decade ago, the Al-Amar Club was formed in Albuquerque. Part social and part charitable, the club now numbers about seventy-five families. *Al-Amar* means "moon" in Arabic ("a romantic symbol of Lebanon," explains one insider). A celebratory meeting called a *hafli* is usually held twice a year. In the winter, there is a blowout at one of the large Albuquerque hotels run by Lebanese families: the Four Seasons or the Classic. In the summer, a picnic is held in the Sandia Mountains or on the State Fairgrounds in Albuquerque. Both events are open to the public. A number of Al-Amar members, such as George

Samara and Salim Hamrah, are not from pioneer households but rather have come to New Mexico within the last thirty to forty years.

To attend a *hafli* is to witness a variegated experience. There is bound to be belly dancing, as well as Lebanese folk dancing called *debka*. Someone will most likely sing "Mejana," a well-known Old Country tune and a favorite of television's Danny Thomas (yes, he's Lebanese, too). The menu features *kibbe*, a ground lamb dish; *tabulleh*, a summer salad; Lebanon Mountains bread, and *ouzo*, a potent anise-flavored aperitif. Afterward, Peter Koury and Al Akgulian of Albuquerque will play the *oud*, a pear-shaped instrument that resembles a mandolin, and which no *hafli* would be without.

At 8,000 feet, Peñasco is at nearly the same altitude as the Lebanon Mountains. There is one big difference between the places, notes Pete Sahd, who lives in Taos County's Peñasco. Sahd says that while his community is abundant in piñon trees, in the hills of Lebanon you can't see the forest for the cedars.

An effusive, mustachioed gent, Sahd opened his you-name-it-we-got-it Peñasco general store in 1947. But his family goes way, way back. His grandfather, Abdo Yussef, came to Las Vegas in 1892. "He sent back to Lebanon for a picture of his wife," says Sahd, sweeping the floor of his store. "When it arrived in Vegas, someone else received it and promptly sold it for fifty dollars. He claimed the photograph was the Virgin Mary, the patron saint of Lebanon."

Born in Roumieh in 1911, Sahd came to the United States when he was eight. He was reared in Cerrillos, New Mexico, a mining center where his father had set up a retail shop. After graduating from the University of New Mexico, Sahd taught school in Golden and Stanley. Following service in the Navy, Sahd turned north toward Peñasco. "I wanted to get away from everything," Sahd says, putting down his broom and removing his apron. Instead of teaching, he started a store in a building that resembles an ancient airplane hangar. He sells everything from butter to bathtubs.

Sahd's father died in 1948. He influenced his son greatly. "Dad loved this country. He wanted to become an American citizen the minute he could—and he did. Dad was not like a lot of Lebanese men. He was easygoing, he enjoyed life. He didn't care if he made a million or not. To him, America was everything. He loved baseball, though he never saw a game. Dad reared me on that—sports and patriotism. Don't get me wrong, I love where I came from. But I don't believe in this hyphenated stuff: Lebanese-American. The Al-Amar thing isn't for me. I'm an American, plain and simple."

Patty Sahd, Pete's wife, isn't Lebanese. But like many wives who aren't, she has learned to make such dishes as *kibbe*. She has also accompanied her husband to the Old Country half a dozen times. On one trip she returned with a big, four-legged brass charcoal brazier used in many homes in Lebanon as a hand warmer. It now sits in the Sahds' living room. "Tell him what *Sahd* means in Arabic," says Patty to her husband. "It means happy, fortunate," says Pete. "That's how I feel about living in this country."

There were three significant characteristics among *los Arabes*. Families were often large, often interrelated, and often serious about religion. Richard Michael of Albuquerque is a member of the widespread Michael clan. His father, Aziz Michael, journeyed to New Mexico in 1890. Later, Aziz was joined by brothers Rashid and Merhege. Aziz fathered twelve children, Merhege, eleven, and Rashid, ten.

Not every New Mexico Lebanese is a blood relative; it just seems that way. However, most of the Michaels in northern New Mexico, most of the Fidels, the Francises, Kourys, Richards, Adelos, Hanoshes, and Sahds are cousins, mostly because they came from Roumieh. The Hindis and the Budaghers, who don't come from Roumieh; found a way to become kin in the United States: Shafei Hindi is married to Emma Budagher.

Once the daughter of a Lebanese was expected to wed only a young man of similar lineage. Rose Fidel Hanosh of Mora met her husband, John, in New Mexico in the 1920s through an Old Country *sinsar*, or matchmaker. That kind of convention has pretty well ceased, though young Brahin Hindi Jr. says when an elderly Lebanese aunt visited Duran a few years ago, the woman had spouses picked out for every Hindi child.

Almost all *los Arabes* were Catholic. In their homeland, they belonged to the Maronite rite. "Old-timers," says Rose Hanosh, "were good Christians. We're biblical people, see, and we relied on our faith a lot in the early days here. This land was pretty rough then. Lots of *misbahas* [rosaries] were said." In Las Vegas, Lebanese went and still go to Our Lady of Sorrows Church in Old Town; in Pecos, St. Anthony's; in Albuquerque, St. Mary's. Since Mass was usually delivered in Spanish in smaller New Mexico churches in those and other places, most Lebanese spoke that language before English. (Because he grew up with Santo Domingo Pueblo Indians, John Budagher's first tongue was Keres.)

One of the first non-Catholic families to caravan to New Mexico was the Hindis. They were Moslem. Islamic mosques being somewhat rare in Torrance County, the Hindis soon dropped their religion. A few family members do attend St. John the Baptist Catholic Church in Duran, but not many. Says Sam Hindi, "Long ago Dad had an argument with the priest there, and that pretty much finished it for all of us. If you're Lebanese, you do what your father says."

One way *los Arabes* became an integral part of New Mexico was to run for public office, mostly as Democrats. Sam Adelo's father was a state senator from San Miguel County. John Budagher's son serves as one from Bernalillo County, as does Valencia County's Joseph Fidel. Basheer (young Bill) Hindi was a state representative from Torrance County. Albert Michael was mayor of Grants. Merhege Michael was a county commissioner, Bud Budagher a county sheriff. Lee Francis, a former rancher from Cubero, rose the highest in politics. Francis was lieutenant governor in the late 1960s. But it was in his genes— his father, Narciso, served in the House of Representatives. And *his* father, Elias, was a diplomat of sorts. Elias Francis was perhaps the first Lebanese to set foot in New Mexico. He came to Seboyeta, near the Laguna Indian Reservation, in 1888.

Kahlil Gibran would be happy to learn that many third- and fourth-generation Lebanese are, like well-aligned arrows, following the path of their forefathers. Brahin Hindi's boy, Jamail, and Nabay Hindi's son, Nabay Alex, have moved onto the Hindi sheep ranch. The signs are good that both young men will make their future there. Gavin and Joe Maloof, George's two eldest boys, still in their twenties, have picked up the reins of their father's conglomerate. Pete Sahd's son, Randy, helps his dad with the Peñasco store, as do Pauline Michael's sons, Edward and James, in Bibo. Where there is a job to be done, where there are opportunities, there will always be *los Arabes*.

Behind the Lines

"This is the field," says Norman Cleaveland, nodding at a meadow choked with chamisa, "where Mother was surrounded by the Indians. You remember. She was about twelve or thirteen, and she was on her horse when those Indians circled her. Mother didn't know what to think. The thing was, the Indians had never seen blond hair. It's all in the book."

Nearly 100 years ago, a young mother and her three small children crossed the San Agustin Plains of central New Mexico in a battered, horse-drawn wagon. When the pioneers, sort of a Swiss Family Robinson minus a father, reached what is now tiny Datil, fifty-five miles west of Socorro, they carved out a life raising cattle on some of the most jagged land known to man. Fifty years later, one of those children—the blond girl stared at by the Indians—carved out a nonfiction book based mainly on that experience and others growing up in rural New Mexico at the turn of the century. Since it first appeared in 1941, Agnes Morley Cleaveland's *No Life for a Lady* has charmed readers with its blend of backwoods adventure and folksy philosophy. Most New Mexico bibliophiles consider *No Life* a regional classic, one of the four or five best books written about the state.

Norman Cleaveland knows his mother's book like a favorite menu. He has read it dozens of times, rereads it yearly, in fact. And every few weeks he travels from his home in Santa Fe to the isolated Datil ranch where the book is set. Here he checks on things, shows the high, dry canyons to visitors, and walks the valleys his mother walked. Cleaveland has returned this day, driving not a wagon such as his mother rode in, but a sleek, silver BMW. At eighty-four, he is a sturdy, erect, regal-looking man with large hands and the voice of a klaxon. "Up in those mountains," Cleaveland blares, gesturing west to a purple ridge, "Mother hunted grizzly bears with Montague Stevens. She and Stevens got rimrocked on a ledge. You remember; it's in the book."

The book. Mrs. Cleaveland penned some western tales prior to her classic. And save for a single other lesser effort, she wrote nothing afterward. "She had one big story in her," says her son, "and she got it out." The book emerged when Mrs. Cleaveland dictated to a typist accounts of her youth: riding sidesaddle across the range alone at night, chasing cattle, being chased by badmen. "It was amazing the way Mother wrote it," says Cleaveland, easing his BMW past a gulley. "The stories came tumbling out in six months. There were no real drafts."

At New Mexico novelist Conrad Richter's urging, Mrs. Cleaveland sent her words to Houghton Mifflin Company in Boston. The publisher liked them and summoned the author, who was then in her sixties, back East for editing. The editing turned out to be mostly cutting; Mrs. Cleaveland's dictated prose proved remarkably graceful. "Lucid" is how her son puts it. Here's a sample: "So many shades of green . . . lavender desert verbena, scarlet patches of Indian paintbrush, great blotches of yellow snakeweed. And above it a turquoise sky with white wooly thunderheads resting upon the mountain peaks."

Cleaveland says his mother titled her manuscript—he can't remember what she called it—but that Houghton Mifflin came up with the phrase that stuck. "Mother liked theirs a whole lot better." The publisher divided the book into forty-five chapters and added little drawings to preface each. *No Life for a Lady* made the bestseller lists nationally, though it never climbed to first place. "Topnotch Americana," cooed a *New Yorker* magazine critic. Through several printings the book sold more than 20,000 copies. Mrs. Cleaveland, a fine speaker, needed no encouragement from Houghton Mifflin to travel the country to promote her opus. During World War II, the armed services published an edition for GIs, as they did with many works of literature. "I stumbled across a copy on an airfield in Alaska," says Cleaveland. The book sold well in England and was translated into German and Swedish. In 1974, William Gannon, a Santa Fe publisher, issued a cloth reprint that sold out quickly. Three years later, the University of Nebraska Press came out with the first and only paperback edition. Four printings later, more than 18,000 copies of that version have been sold. *No Life for a Lady* continues to sell well. "Mother didn't make a fortune from the book," says her son, "but she did okay."

Entering a shady glen known as Wood Spring Flat, Cleaveland stops alongside a stone marker. The grave holds the ashes of Ray Morley, Mrs. Cleaveland's younger brother. Second to the author, Morley received the most ink of anyone in *No Life for a Lady*. Mrs. Cleaveland devoted one chapter and parts of several more to her brother. When the two siblings weren't scrapping, they worked to survive in a wild place. Often they drew on a wacky sense of humor. Morley, his sister recalled in the book, once staged a fake gunfight to scare a tenderfoot off the ranch. Later, Morley played football at Columbia University and then settled on the ranch, where he developed into a legendary storyteller and practical joker. He dyed sheep he owned different colors and then passed the animals off to tourists as alien strains.

Morley died in 1932 at age fifty-six. "He had a bad heart," says Cleaveland, cleaning his glasses with a handkerchief. "Doctors told him this altitude wasn't good and sent him to California, to sea level. Ray hated every minute out there; Datil was his home." Morley died in a Pasadena, California, hotel, not of heart trouble, says his nephew, but of a broken heart.

Steering his car down a slope, Cleaveland brakes beside a trail head. "In the book, Mother talks about a Mrs. Manning and her four-year-old son, who had never seen any playmates. Well, one day she took me up to play with him—right up that trail there—and you'll remember we fought like the dickens." (Here's how the author put it: "The two boys flew at each other like a couple of cub wildcats.")

After *No Life for a Lady* came out, some Catron County old-timers approached Mrs. Cleaveland and grumbled, "Hey, that's not the way it was." Eyeing them sternly, the author replied, "Well, that's the way it coulda been."

Cleaveland pauses in front of a bare bluff. "The school where Mother taught stood right here. You remember; it's in the book. Mother was sixteen at the time. She was paid with eggs. One of her students was Gus Wheeler. He was the lad who toted six-guns and did target practice during recess."

In its heyday, the Datil ranch covered more than a half-million acres. After Ray Morley's death, most of the working ranch was sold. A portion of it is now owned by a family from Austin, Texas.

Turning his car around, Cleaveland drives some more, then halts in front of a double-wide mobile home on a corner of the ranch that has remained in the Cleaveland family. Cleaveland stays in the trailer whenever he returns to Datil to check on things. Inside the mobile home are photographs of Cleaveland's grandparents (his mother's mother died in Datil in 1917; her husband was shot in Mexico before she moved to Catron County). There are photos of Uncle Ray, Aunt Lora (the third Morley child), old Mac, a horse Mrs. Cleaveland rode through the pages of *No Life*, and a sketch of the White House, the family's first Datil home, long since gone.

Between sips of coffee, Cleaveland says he was born in 1901, not on the ranch, as might be expected, but in California, where his mother lived periodically. Cleaveland, however, spent parts of his childhood in Datil. His earliest memory of the place is of accompanying his mother on a horse and having a badger jump in front of them. As a young man, Cleaveland returned to California to attend school. "My father, Newton Cleaveland, was an engineer, a meticulous man. He'd grown up in California and his work was there. He didn't care much for New Mexico. Mother, on the other hand, loved New Mexico. She loved being on a horse, and she was daring and independent and rebellious. Somehow they kept their marriage together for years—even when she lived in Datil and he stayed in California. By the way, my father was very proud of the book."

Curiously, Norman Cleaveland became a celebrity before his mother did. A football star at Stanford University under coach "Pop" Warner, Cleaveland nearly made the Rose Bowl. In 1924, he earned a gold medal in rugby at the Paris Olympics. Like his father, Cleaveland became a mining engineer and did well. He spent twenty-two years in Malaya dredging tin. Like his mother, he wrote a book about his life and times. It's titled *Bang! Bang! in Ampang*. Says the author: "It didn't cause much of a stir." Almost twenty years ago, Cleaveland retired to Santa Fe, where he resides with his sister, Loraine Lavender, who holds the copyright to *No Life*. Divorced, Cleaveland has three grown children who live in England. They come to Datil occasionally, and yes, all have read their grandmother's book several times.

Rising, Cleaveland returns to his car for one last spin around the ranch. "Up there," he says, nodding toward a big, pine-covered hump, "is Swingle Hill. You remember Billy Swingle from the book, don't you? A real character. Preferred to sleep outdoors year-round. That mountain over there is Rustler's Hill. Mother crossed it one time and met some thieves on the dodge. They didn't do anything to her because they saw she was a girl."

Motioning toward still one more mountain, Cleaveland says it was there that faith healer Francis Schlatter wanted to start a second Jerusalem. In the book, Schlatter is a man of spiritual intrigue. "Mother always looked upon that mountain reverentially," says Cleaveland, idling his car engine, "so much so that my sister began to call it Mount Fuji. Mother didn't like that name very much."

In the mid-1950s, Mrs. Cleaveland went to California for eye and hip surgery. "It wasn't very successful," says her son. Mrs. Cleaveland wanted to return to Datil, perhaps for the last time, but her doctors said no; her health seemed too frail. Then, remembering her brother and how he had died so far from his roots, Mrs. Cleaveland coerced her West Coast physicians into letting her board a train. By the time she arrived in Albuquerque, she had taken a turn for the worse and was rushed to Presbyterian Hospital. Her hip pained her greatly, and her failing eyesight had sent her into a deep depression.

Cleaveland, then living in Malaya, raced back to New Mexico. "When I got to the hospital, Mother was in bad shape. I asked her what I could do for her. She said, 'Get me to Datil.' " When two nurses agreed to accompany Mrs. Cleaveland to the ranch in an ambulance, Albuquerque doctors okayed the 2½-hour trip. "Mother lived three more months, all here," says her son, tapping his fingers on the steering wheel. "She was happy. Surely she wouldn't have lived that long anywhere else. This was her home."

Agnes Morley Cleaveland died at Datil on March 7, 1958. She was eighty-three. Her ashes lie atop "Mount Fuji," facing the canyons and meadows she loved so well and wrote about so memorably in the book.

Home, Sweet House

The gnarled cowpoke over there by the iced-tea table? That's Sam Blackburn. Sam came to House when he was ten; he's eighty-nine now. Sam has been around town so long he's, well, a household word.

That perky gal in the gingham frock? Opal Whitfield. Opal motored up from Kermit, Texas, to this year's homecoming. She'd come a lot farther, she says, to thank House for what it gave her. When she lived here, when her mother was, well, a housewife, Opal studied dramatics over to the old school. Learned to use my mouth, is how Opal puts it. The skill brought her success: Opal's now one of the nation's leading storm-door salespeople.

The big-bellied, black-bearded fellow in the short-sleeve plain shirt? Looks kinda like Wolfman Jack, don't he? He's Mike Weigl, now of Gallup. Mike was born here fifty years ago. Old Doc Herring delivered him. Mike has always liked to eat, ever since he stole watermelons as a kid. Heck, Mike just about ate his folks out of, well, you get the idea.

An Open House

Each year since 1975, more than 200 people—from aging pioneers to brave newcomers—have shown up for the annual homecoming at

House, a wide space on the high plains forty miles south of Tucumcari. The yearly House party is lots of things: it's dusting off a semi-clean straw chapeau and cinching a skillet-size belt buckle. It's getting a perm and putting on a shirt with marble thumbtack buttons. And it's spoofing. *Question*: Were you born in House? *Answer*: Nope. In hospital.

A farming and ranching outpost, House is one of those east-side settlements that boomed at the turn of the century, thanks to Texas homesteaders, and then, in the early 1950s, began to die like a severed limb.

Early on, 2,000 people called House home. A dozen stores edged four busy dirt streets. Three hundred students arrived at the community school each day. Currently, House has fewer than 200 souls, 90 pupils in 12 grades, and a single grocery. Most of the streets are still dirt.

House Hunting

House is not an easy place to find. The sign in front of the cemetery is larger than the sign in front of the town. When a couple of obviously lost strangers wandered into House a while back, Stanley Martin, a genuine spoofer, sent them over to the Baptist Church.

Despite the town's remoteness, people from everywhere find their way to the House Community Center one weekend each spring. Bob Mead and his wife, Joanne, got up this year at 4:00 A.M. and drove down from Taos, where they raise Angus cattle. Chris Schroeder came to this year's homecoming from Germany. Well, actually, Chris is a foreign exchange student at the local high school. Folks in House have grown fond of Chris. He has taught them all sorts of things, particularly new ways of dressing up. You can't miss Chris; he's leaning against the far wall. Yep, the slender kid wearing the huarache sandals, Saint Laurent shades, parachute pants, and spiked hair.

A check of signatures in the homecoming guest book shows certain names appearing again and again: Runyan, Blackburn, Snipes. A gracious little white-haired woman owns two of those names. Opal Snipes Blackburn is class of '33 at House. Forty-five years later she served as mayor. She says she didn't become mayor for the glory, but to help the ailing little community. Opal got a lot done during her four-year term. She organized a library, a medical facility, and the rodeo grounds. Then Opal moved to Clovis.

A Pox on This House

Nobody who lived in House during the 1950s has completely happy memories. A severe drought that started in 1949 continued for seven consecutive years. Blowing sand burned House's grasslands bunny brown. Wheat fields turned to chalk. President Eisenhower flew over to take a look; he flew away shaking his head. Before the fifties, most House farmers worked a quarter section. The drought and rising prices drove small farmers out of Quay County. Only the bigger ones survived.

Fact is, it has never been easy to live in House. Original colonists John and Lucie House spent the first months of 1902 in a tent. Gay Morris Blair—she's standing over there in the pink dress by the pastries—used to live only three miles from town, but her meandering bus trip to school covered twenty miles. Bud Snipes—he's the rangy-looking guy waiting in line for more fried chicken—used to run to school each day during track season. Eleven miles each way.

Good Housekeeping

Troubled or not, House has a way of drawing back its own to the cap rock. Sure there was that interminable dry spell, the flood of '37, and a scarlet fever epidemic. But there also were the wonderful box dinners and singing conventions. Those events are what old-timers remember and why so many of them reappear at homecoming.

For recent arrivals, the town's three churches and an active 4-H group offer friendly faces. And there's always television: the windmills may be gone, but satellite dishes are here to stay. So are barns, thank goodness. A farm without an animal house makes as much sense as a sailor without a ship.

They Played Like a House Afire

That white-haired gentleman in the wheelchair holding court in the vestibule is certainly someone you want to meet. Creighton Brown's his name, '23's his class. For seventeen years Brown taught and coached at House. For several years the school had no gym; Brown's basketball teams played on a court outdoors. Surely Brown's greatest achievement came in 1938, when House won the state basketball championship. That was an era when high schools were not broken into divisions; everyone, no matter how teeny, played everyone else. House that year fielded a grand team: they had Charles Halbert, a six-foot, ten-inch monster who later had a cup of coffee with the semipro Peoria Caterpillars. At state, little House beat Clovis, Las Cruces, and Hobbs. In the championship game, the House Cowboys skewered the Gallup Bengals by twenty points. Indoors.

There Is a Doctor From This House

Over in the spanking-new House School home ec room, the class of 1935 is holding a fifty-year reunion in conjunction with the town's homecoming. There were eleven in that class, and all but two have come back. One student died in World War II. The other absentee is Bazil Highly. Pride fills the voices of Bazil's old school chums when they speak of him. Bazil, who never married, lives way out in Hollywood, California. No, he isn't in the movies or anything like that. Bazil works as a tree surgeon. Gets $1,500 to clip a gingko, someone says.

Another star of that class has shown up. Of course, Elizabeth Henson Wortman admits she had only to come over from Lubbock, Texas. Elizabeth has written a novel for teen-agers titled *To Babylon and Back Again*. It's about a young girl growing up in, of all places, Mountainair, New Mexico.

Down the hall from the home ec room, class pictures dominate several walls. There are big classes: in 1941, twenty-two students graduated. In 1976, three. This year eight students received diplomas. There are famous graduates: the class of 1955 included Glen Franklin, who became a world champion calf roper. And there are familiar graduates: Elton Kirchmeier served as president of the class of 1944. The vice president that year was Marylea Kirchmeier, Elton's bride.

Bless This House

Standing in the men's room of the new school, one ex-resident, in town for homecoming, notes that when he lived in House, five decades before, things were a lot less fancy. For instance, indoor plumbing wasn't even available. Why, students and just about everybody else in these parts had to walk outside, usually around back. Got the idea?

A Textbook Case

The call came just as the open-faced console clock showed 4:46 A.M. in the windowless dispatcher's room on South Coors Road in Albuquerque. Veronica Espiñosa, at work that Tuesday morning July 29, 1980, carefully recorded the time in the Bernalillo County Fire Department's big log book, and beside it, an alarm number— 1225— the 1,225th alarm of the year. Before putting down her pencil, Espiñosa was able to get an address: 7325 Isleta Southwest, at the far end of Albuquerque's South Valley.

Because the fire was in District Four, at 4:47 A.M., Frank Atencio, the other dispatcher on duty, contacted the station house at Isleta Boulevard and Barcelona Road. Seconds later he rang the station at Isleta and Margo Road. Then the one at Five Points. Later, someone figured out that twelve fire units were sent into the cool gray dawn. Nobody ever figured out who turned in the alarm.

In his West Mesa home, Chris Archuleta moved with a start when his bedside telephone sounded at 5:31 A.M. One of three arson inspectors for the Bernalillo County Fire Department, Archuleta was on twenty-four-hour call. Any time there was a major fire, or one of a suspicious nature, an arson inspector was automatically summoned. At 5:47 A.M., Archuleta arrived at the fire scene—the old, nearly abandoned Los Padillas School, at the corner of Isleta and Los Padillas

Road. A group of people in nightclothes had already surrounded the burning T-shaped structure. One glance at the blaze told Archuleta the building couldn't be saved. Walking about the scene, he began to question onlookers. Strangely, as distraught as many were about the fire, none wanted to talk. Again and again people would shake their heads when Archuleta asked for information.

At 6:14 A.M., Bill Hoefler, fire chief of District Four, cornered the arson inspector. Hoefler confided that two of the firemen on the scene early had some things to report, some things, said Hoefler, that were strange. Fireman Nick Napoleone had been first to enter the burning building. He had pried open one of the double doors on the west side of the school. Quickly peering down a flaming hallway, Napoleone had spotted, about fifteen to twenty feet away, a small puddle in the center of the floor. Another fireman, George Woodard, told Archuleta that when he had gone in the school's unlocked front door, which faced east, he had noticed a heavy concentration of flames close to the floor.

Just as arson inspectors are trained to use their noses, they are also taught to read fire patterns. The two reports told Chris Archuleta that an accelerant had probably been used to burn down the old Los Padillas School.

Despite the number of fire trucks present, this was not an easy fire to put out. The main problem was lack of water. Most of the fire districts in Albuquerque's South Valley do not have hydrants. Water has to be shuttled in by tanker trucks. Nearly 150,000 gallons were eventually used for this blaze. Additionally, the fire had begun in the worst place to fight it: the center of the building. "Even if we had been right across the street when it started," Bill Hoefler said later, "we probably wouldn't have been able to stop it from destroying the building."

By 7:50 A.M., the fire was under control. By 10:15 A.M., it was extinguished, though nearly forty-eight hours later it continued to smolder. By 9:30 A.M., Chris Archuleta had left for an appointment involving another case. During the next few hours, however, he could not get this fire out of his thoughts: "So much fuss over a decrepit schoolhouse, yet so little cooperation as to what might have happened. Why?" He sensed this was going to be a difficult case.

Archuleta was a quiet, articulate young man with a well-groomed mustache. Only twenty-three, he had been a county arson inspector for five months. Before that he was a fireman for three years, a job he liked but not as much as his present one. He had investigated 120 arson cases. Since joining the arson squad, Archuleta had embraced his work with enthusiasm. He had taken arson courses in Colorado and West Virginia. He was a member of the International Association of Arson Investigators and was secretary-treasurer of the New Mexico chapter. He spoke earnestly of arson being a growing crime, one that increases 25 percent to 30 percent each year, one that annually costs Americans $15 billion in damages, not to mention loss of lives. But it wasn't the seriousness of the crime alone that drew Archuleta to this line of work. "Arson investigation is a challenge," he explained. "Your evidence is burned up."

At 1:08 P.M., Archuleta returned to the fire site. By 3:05 P.M., the fire had cooled down enough for him to take his first sample. He got it from the hall area where Nick Napoleone had spotted the pool of liquid. Digging in the rubble, Archuleta scooped up several handfuls of ash and put them into a one-gallon can. The following morning he took the can to a laboratory run by the Albuquerque Fire Department.

Over the next several days, while he waited for the lab results, Archuleta, as a policeman might, knocked on doors. The settlement of Los Padillas dates back to 1705, a year before Albuquerque's birth. The name of the community, as well as the name of the old school, derives from Juan Padilla, a priest and founder of an orphanage for children whose parents were killed by Navajos. Padilla himself eventually met the same fate. It is believed his orphanage stood on the old school site. Though it has grown to about 7,500 residents, Los Padillas has changed only slightly since its namesake's time. Farming is still the chief occupation. Dozens of placards along this stretch of Isleta Boulevard advertise chile for sale. If there has been one real change, it's the appearance of several NO TRESPASSING signs. Privacy in Los Padillas is valued nearly as much as the next melon crop.

As Archuleta suspected, his door knocking turned up nothing; people still were not talking. "They seem afraid" Archuleta thought. "Afraid their own house might get burned down." Archuleta was sure somebody had seen something. If no one was talking to Archuleta, they were talking to Crime Stoppers. At 9:00 A.M. on July 29, only four hours after the blaze was reported, Crime Stoppers received a call on the fire. Four more unsolicited telephone calls about the fire were taken that day. During the following week and a half, three suspects emerged from the calls. All three were from Los Padillas, and all three were male. One was a juvenile. Each was asked to come down to the county fire marshal's office for questioning.

Experience had taught Archuleta that interrogation should be

done at eye level. To be looked down upon, he felt, might cause intim-
idation, which in turn could bring wrongful testimony. Wearing a
gun, he knew, had the same effect. Unlike Albuquerque Fire Department arson inspectors, Archuleta was not armed. The interrogations
got nowhere, however. All three suspects had alibis for the early hours
of July 29. Though he had a strong hunch about one suspect, Archuleta
sensed if he pushed too hard he might blow the case. He simply had
to wait for more facts.

In any presumed arson case looms the profit motive. Fifteen percent of all incendiaries each year are done to swindle insurance companies. The old Los Padillas School was owned by Bernalillo County.
Though it had most recently been used as a meal site for senior citizens, as a school Los Padillas had not been active for fifteen years
and was in decay. Still, the building was valued at $470,000, insured
by the county through Wausau Merchants Property Company. Coincidentally, two days before the fire, the county had received a federal
grant of $189,000 to help renovate the structure. In one piece or anoth-
er the property was worth something.

On July 30, the day after the fire, Michael Hering, a Minneapolis
private investigator, arrived in Albuquerque. He had been sent by Wausau. Hering spent from 8:00 A.M. till 3:00 P.M. that day at the fire
site. He took an ash sample. He knocked on doors. Then he met with
Archuleta. Arson inspectors and insurance investigators have always
had an uneasy relationship. Though a man like Hering was only concerned with finding fraud—he was not going to prosecute anyone—
he represented competition. No professional, not even one as amiable
as Archuleta, likes someone looking over his shoulder. What then
did Hering and Archuleta talk about? "We discussed how he could
get my lab report and how I could get his," said Archuleta later. Then,
with a faint smile, Archuleta added: "He couldn't find anyone in the
neighborhood who would talk, either."

On August 6, Carolyn Romero, chemist for the Albuquerque Fire
Department, completed the lab report on Archuleta's ash sample. The
report stated: "Chromatographic analysis of pentane extracts reveal
the presence of a few lower boiling point components which are insig-
nificant for identification purposes." Translation: something was used
to start the fire but what it was cannot be ascertained.

Archuleta was greatly disappointed. During the next two and a
half weeks he ran down the alibis the three suspects had provided.
Another dead end; all checked out. "In other cases," said Archuleta,
"if you had talked to as many persons as I had, you would have solved

this. Eventually you would have found someone who had heard something. Not here. Our trouble wasn't that the lab report was weak. Our trouble was that nobody was talking."

On August 27, Archuleta contacted the state office of Crime Stoppers. He hoped it might yield more facts. On September 10, that agency announced a $1,000 reward for information about the fire. The notice was sent to fifty radio stations and thirty-seven newspapers. There were no responses. "Whoever did the fire is not bragging about it," reasoned Greg MacAleese, who ran Crime Stoppers' state office. "The person (or persons) is keeping quiet, which is somewhat odd." Archuleta had his own theories. He believed the arsonist was not young. Juveniles, he knew, usually did sloppy jobs. This one was a good job—the gasoline, or whatever accelerant was used, was spread around. And in all the right places. But what Archuleta couldn't figure out was why someone would torch a harmless old building. The only answer he could come up with was revenge. Perhaps a former student at the school held a grudge.

On September 3, Michael Hering telephoned Archuleta. Hering's ash sample had come back from the lab negative. Wausau would probably be paying.

Not everyone who lived in Los Padillas was close-mouthed. If Archuleta had a counterpart in that region of Albuquerque's South Valley, if there was someone as interested as he in flushing out the arsonist, it was Josephine Turrietta. A forthright, winsome woman who wore her sixty-five years well, Josie Turrietta had arrived in Los Padillas in 1943 from Albuquerque's North Valley. She had come to Los Padillas to marry Frank Turrietta, a widower who lived on Isleta Boulevard with four young daughters. Frank Turrietta, who was now retired, had been, ironically, a fireman for many years at Sandia National Laboratories. He was also a graduate of the old school, class of 1910.

That Josie Turrietta was not a true native of the neighborhood perhaps explained her willingness to discuss the case and its ramifications. During her thirty-seven years in Los Padillas, Turrietta had come to love the area. Why? "Because I like people and I like to preserve what our ancestors gave us. And this is what I found in Los Padillas—a grand tradition." Farms, groceries, all kinds of small businesses in Los Padillas are passed from one generation to the next. Turrietta said it was important to understand that these were clannish folk; many were related. "Not many," she corrected herself.

"Everybody—the Sanchezes, the Montoyas, the Padillas—everybody is related to everybody else." Turietta didn't state it but her tone was clear: you live in Los Padillas, you don't rat on your *primo*, or cousin.

If there is—was—one grand tradition in the Los Padillas neighborhood, it was the old school. Immediately after she relocated to the area, Josie Turrietta became involved with it. She spearheaded the PTA, cooked enchilada suppers for the teachers, and swept and cleaned the building regularly. And the more she became involved, the more she became impressed by the school's roots. The original Los Padillas School was a one-roomer constructed in 1901. Until July 29, 1980, the school was the only building of historic importance still standing in the neighborhood, the oldest remaining school building in the Rio Abajo.

Various alterations had been made to the structure over the years. Six rooms were added in 1912, at which time the *Albuquerque Journal* proclaimed Los Padillas to have "the most modern school in New Mexico." Built mostly of *terrones* in Mission style, with Romanesque and Gothic influences, the school was a period piece, a colorful and curious architectural monument.

Being a landmark wasn't enough to keep the place from being a target for destruction. In 1964, a year before the new Los Padillas Elementary School opened a half-mile away, vandals broke into the old building and started a fire that caused $14,000 in damage. In recent years, graffiti scarred the school's walls. Windows were broken repeatedly. Somehow, the school weathered each storm, even 1979's county proposal to bring in the wrecking ball. Certain bureaucrats said the school had become an eyesore, a nuisance to the neighborhood. It should be torn down. Outraged at such an idea, Josie Turrietta and a few other Los Padillas residents worked tirelessly to gain funds that would help fix up the building. A large grant from the Heritage Conservation and Recreation Service came through finally. It would turn the aging structure into a community center. A grand tradition would be saved. Then came the morning of July 29.

It was 4:55 A.M. when Josie Turrietta answered her kitchen telephone and heard her good friend Agapita Cordova shouting hysterically on the other end. "Calm down, calm down," said a sleepy Turrietta. "Mia Dios! Mia Dios!" sobbed Mrs. Cordova. "The old school . . . it is burning."

Her heart thumping madly, Josie Turrietta raced down Isleta Boulevard in the darkness. Her mind spun. "Am I dreaming?" she wondered. No. In the distance she could see the flames. "I cried till I was blue in the face," Turietta remembered. "It made me sick, disgusted. All the work and effort in two seconds went down the drain."

Blood may be thicker than water in Los Padillas, but Turrietta said that contrary to what some outsiders believe, people there do care. She witnessed that during the fire. Simon Padilla, who lived on nearby Malpais Road, helped haul water from his own well to the fire. Teresa Padilla, who resided across the street from where the school once stood, brought coffee to the firemen. These two and many others had attended the school as children; their memories were strong. Turrietta said to see the school disappear was to watch a living thing die.

With each passing day, Chris Archuleta grew more frustrated. Because of a shortage of arson inspectors and an overload of cases, he could not give alarm number 1225 his undivided attention. Even if he could, he doubted he would find out much more.

Though few persons in Los Padillas talked excitedly about it, plans were still under way to build a community center. Erecting the center was made easier in one way: there was nothing left on the old school site. On August 2, 1980, five dump trucks and two steam shovels from the Bernalillo County Road Department began removal of what remained—charred walls, parts of radiators, ceiling beams, some chair legs. Workers carted the debris to a city landfill on South Broadway. The old school survived nearly eighty years. It took eight men working two days to bury it.

The case of the Los Padillas School fire remains unsolved. "It's still a great mystery," says Josie Turrietta. The Los Padillas Community Center was dedicated July 18, 1982.

Close Encounter

Lonnie Zamora has lived at the same address in Socorro since 1948. The small, white stucco house Zamora built when he got married is located in the southwest part of town, on an unpaved road that is difficult to find: there is no street sign. Yet for the last twenty years people have somehow found Zamora's home. After circling the Lujan Funeral Parlor several times, and then passing the nearby cemetery once or twice, the inquisitive frequently give up and ask, though not at the graveyard, "Where does that guy who saw the flying saucer live?"

A few neighbors who know Zamora well occasionally pretend they have no idea where he lives. Sometimes the curious are even sent on wild-goose chases. Folks in Socorro do these things because they know that Zamora doesn't like to talk about what happened in the early evening of April 24, 1964. "Lonnie's had it up to here," says one friend. Zamora, in fact, only gives interviews when the mood strikes him. And in recent years the mood has not struck. However, not long ago, Zamora did agree to talk. His explanation was that if he did, the whole mess might finally go away.

Zamora is a short man, about five feet, seven inches tall. He is solidly built, in the manner of someone who has done physical labor. His wrists and forearms are thick, his hands large and calloused. His thinning gray hair is worn in what must be one of the last flattops in Socorro County. As he sits in the paneled living room of his home, Zamora speaks slowly, choosing his words carefully. When he talks, a gold-capped front tooth glistens. But he doesn't talk often. Zamora has always been a man who prefers to listen. As he listens, he cracks his knuckles repeatedly. "What did I see?" Zamora says in a polite but somewhat bored voice. "It was more frightening than anything that could happen. If you're a policeman, which I was back then, and you get in a gun battle, you're scared. But once it's over, it's over. This you can't forget."

What Zamora has never quite forgotten is what he has always contended he saw in a deserted arroyo south of Socorro: a shiny, oval-shaped vehicle and two small, peculiar-looking figures dressed in white coveralls. The event occurred at 5:50 P.M. on a Friday. At the time, Zamora was an officer with the Socorro Police Department. Alone in his patrol car, he was following a speeder north on California Avenue, Socorro's main thoroughfare, when he heard behind him and to his left, a "loud noise, like an explosion." Glancing back, he says, he glimpsed for a moment in the distance a "shooting flame." Ignoring the speeder, Zamora braked, turned his police car around and rushed to the area that had attracted him—a deserted, shrub-studded arroyo about a mile from downtown.

As his white Pontiac bounded over a gravel path, Zamora viewed in the distance what he said appeared to be an overturned car. Leaving his own vehicle, the officer saw two figures, "about the size of boys," dressed in white overalls, standing beside an object that looked for all the world like an egg. Protruding from the bottom of the object were girderlike legs. On the side of the craft Zamora spotted an upside-down red V.

As he drew to within 100 feet, Zamora called to the two figures. When they did not answer, the officer retreated to his patrol car, reached in, and grabbed his radio. Excitedly he asked for help. Crouching by his car, not quite understanding what was happening, Zamora suddenly heard a noise, *bing bing*. Another flame appeared and then the object took off, to the southwest, cruising about twenty feet above the ground as it traveled.

From the moment Zamora saw the object until it left was later estimated to be less than two minutes. Yet within a couple of hours the arroyo was swarming with people. The biggest task that authorities faced was to protect evidence of the alleged finding: four indentations in the earth and a scorched greasewood bush. Experts of every stripe peered at that evidence. Teams of Air Force investigators came from White Sands and from Kirtland Air Force Base in Albuquerque. Another Air Force group, experienced investigators of unidentified flying objects (UFOs), jetted in from Ohio. The import of the incident was elevated a notch or two when Dr. J. Allen Hynek arrived in town. A professor of astronomy at Northwestern University, Hynek was recognized as one of the world's foremost UFO researchers.

Since there were no ready explanations for Zamora's sightings and since Zamora seemed so earnest, the story made international news. Though Socorro at the time had about 6,000 residents, the city suddenly became a circled spot on the map. Tourists and flying saucer buffs appeared at the arroyo almost immediately. Within a couple of days, the marks in the earth and the burned greasewood bush were gone: they'd been trampled.

That did not stop people from talking or writing about the event. Zamora's purported encounter became the subject of an entire book and at least two movies. Hynek, who always said he was as baffled as anyone by what happened, nonetheless called the incident "one of the most authenticated landing sightings on record." (Since people have been keeping track, more than 10,000 sightings have been reported.) The Socorro sighting was a major one, though, and as such, nearly every UFO text would include a chapter on it. A "classic case," announced Hynek.

There is little left in Socorro today of that classic case. A fenced-in monument was planned, but it was never built. The Chamber of Commerce, which once considered turning out post cards of Zamora's account, has nearly forgotten it ever took place. Only on a backroom shelf in the chamber's small office is it remembered: in a dusty frame sits a montage of newspaper clippings describing the incident. The two copies of a book written about the event have been swiped from the Socorro Public Library.

James Luckie, seventy-eight, is the retired undersheriff of Socorro County. Luckie was in the police station the evening Zamora radioed, in an agitated voice, this message: "You gotta come out here! You gotta see this to believe!" Luckie was one of the first to arrive at the arroyo. "The bushes were smolderin' like somebody'd cut them from the top with some big flame thrower. Lonnie was white as a corpse and he ain't exactly no paleface normally. He was sweatin' like a spent horse. But it was cold sweat."

Luckie says he asked Zamora what he had seen. "Maybe," answered Zamora, "I seen the devil." Today, Luckie has on the living room wall of his Socorro home a copy of the same framed document tucked away at the Chamber of Commerce. Luckie says the Socorro newspaper manufactured about 100 of the mementoes and sold them for $2.25 each. Because he arrived at the scene early, Luckie was later interviewed by a radio station in Los Angeles. A week after that he received a letter from a UFO investigator in Spain. "One of these days," says Luckie, who has never liked to move too fast, "I'm gonna have to answer that letter."

Two other persons came to the arroyo shortly after Luckie. One was D. Arthur Byrnes, an FBI agent. By coincidence, Byrnes was working in the Socorro police station that day on another matter. Now retired in Albuquerque, Byrnes says he went to the scene in an unofficial capacity. "Lonnie was sitting out there with what might be considered a worried look. I tried comforting him. I was the one who called the people at White Sands. But, hey, whatever happened out there didn't hurt anybody. I always thought about it matter-of-factly."

For eight years, Ted Jordan was stationed at Socorro with the New Mexico State Police. Now retired after twenty-five years with that department, and living in Seminole, Oklahoma, Jordan heard Zamora's radio call, too, and went to the arroyo. He had a thirty-five-millimeter camera with him and shot a roll of film: of four six-inch-deep indentations in the ground, of the scorched bush, and of what Jordan remembers to be "footprints shaped like coffee cups." Jordan says that the following day one of the Air Force investigators asked him for his film. "The dude said he'd give me duplicates," recalls Jordan. "So I handed it over. I forgot all about it until a month or so later. Then I called and asked where was the film. They said, sorry, but my film didn't turn out. They said, and this part always bothered me, that my film had been ruined by radiation."

The troublesome part of all this was that although the impressions in the ground and the seared bush were seen by many, no one saw what Lonnie Zamora said he saw. Hynek, the distinguished UFO consultant, says: "It's really a pity, but no one's fault, that other witnesses did not see the object land or take off." That fact caused Zamora to become a target of skeptics. His character and motives underwent scrutiny. As that began to happen, Zamora withdrew. Crank telephone calls in the night caused him to clam up. Other persons who had followed Zamora to the arroyo experienced the same thing. "I just quit talking about it to every Tom, Dick, and Harry," says James Luckie. "I got tired of being called a damn liar. People would say to me, 'Oh, you're a fool; you never saw nothin.' " Those who knew Zamora well, however, never questioned his story. Says Luckie: "He's a good man, and he was always a good policeman." Hynek calls Zamora "basically sincere and reliable. Not capable of contriving a complex hoax."

Hoax. The word began to pop up as soon as the story broke. After all, the history of UFOs then, as now, is heavy with folks often regarded as kooks. Was Zamora one? Felix Phillips lived four blocks from the arroyo. Phillips told investigators that on the evening of April 24, he was at home and his front door and windows were open to catch the spring breeze. Phillips said he heard nothing. Not at 5:50 P.M.; not at any time.

Did Zamora make up the whole thing? Was he drinking that evening? Was this just another swamp gas mirage, a frequent occurrence elsewhere at the time? Hynek says no way. "I found nothing that tends to discredit Mr. Zamora." Art Byrnes, the ex-FBI agent, rules out alcohol. "I knew Lonnie before that incident, and I never knew him to drink. There was never any indication of narcotics. I always found Lonnie very stable. And Lonnie wouldn't go for a publicity stunt if one were proposed. He's always been too honest."

But the hoax idea would not go away. Philip Klass, a debunker of this case and others, published a book in 1974 titled *UFOs Explained*. Klass suggests that the Socorro event was a scheme to pull the community out of an economic depression. To support his theory, Klass says scientists at Socorro's New Mexico Institute of Mining and Technology, who surely might want to study a UFO sighting in their back yard, seemed totally uninterested. Furthermore, Klass points out that the alleged UFO landed on property owned by Holm Bursum, mayor of Socorro at the time, and a prominent banker. Bursum, contends Klass, would "not be unhappy to see an influx of tourist dollars."

Holm Bursum is no longer mayor of Socorro, but he still lives in the town. He chuckles at Klass's conclusions. "The man is silly. Sure, it was my land where that took place. I went out and took a look like everybody else. And I was excited as everybody else. It was like saying you saw a ghost in a graveyard. But I sure didn't plan it." Bursum discounts the idea that Zamora fabricated the happening. "To my knowledge, Lonnie is not a daydreamer. He's not a practical joker. He's a very serious person and always has been."

A few months after the incident, Ray Senn, city clerk of Socorro, announced that the town was going to try to cash in on its sudden notoriety. When a Hollywood movie company came to Socorro, Senn led them around with relish. When the movie people said they would premiere in Socorro their film about Zamora's sighting, Senn whooped with joy. "Then they told me they wanted $15,000 up front to do that," remembers Senn. "Well, $15,000 was a lot of money in those days. We were babes in the woods. But we weren't that ignorant. We said no." The movie, titled *Phenomenon 7.7*, was shown in parts of the country, though few in Socorro can recollect seeing it, including Senn. Today, the memory of April 24, 1964, and what followed, amuses Senn, except where Zamora is concerned. "If it had been any body else but Lonnie who said they had sighted a UFO, I would have doubted it. Lonnie's just too straight a guy."

"Lonnie's a real fine fella," adds Opal Grinder, once owner of a Whiting Brothers Service Station on Socorro's California Avenue. Grinder remembers another film company, this one a documentary outfit from England, arriving in Socorro. That firm came to his gas station to shoot footage of the owner. "They come to me," says Grinder, "because on the same day, just before Lonnie said he'd heard that noise and saw that flame, a car come into my station. It was a '55 gray Cadillac with Colorado plates. I'll never forget it." Grinder says a man and two small children were riding in the car. The man asked Grinder if there were any funny-looking, low-flying airplanes in the area. Why? wondered Grinder. "Because," the man answered, "one just made a pass at my car down the road. And a police car went tearing after it." Grinder took his story to the Air Force. "They said they would look for the man, but I don't know if they ever did. I advertised for him myself, but I never found him."

With no witnesses to corroborate him, Zamora started giving others the silent treatment. Holm Bursum says he can understand Zamora's reticence. "I think Lonnie just got tired of people coming up and saying, 'What's new on Mars?'"

Zamora's son, Michael, twenty-three, says his father has never talked to him about the incident. "He's a very to-himself person in all ways," Michael says. Zamora's wife, Mary, agrees. "He's quiet. I'm surprised he would talk to you." A tall, slim woman, Mary Zamora works in the records section of the Socorro General Hospital. She has always been a big influence on her husband. After the incident, Zamora could not sleep; he was plagued by nightmares. His wife pressed him into switching to a night shift and to make sure he always had a partner with him on patrol. (On April 24, 1964, Zamora had just left his partner off for dinner when he heard the explosion in the arroyo.)

Working nights did not ease Zamora's pain. Arriving home, he would plop down in a chair in a daze and wonder what he had seen in that arroyo. He would question why he had to be the one to see it. Finally, Mary Zamora urged her husband to visit a priest at San Miguel Mission. "It helped," says Zamora. "The priest told me to stop thinking about it all the time." As close as she is to her husband, Mary Zamora says he has told her little about what he saw in the arroyo. The family keeps no scrapbooks. "All I know," says Mrs. Zamora with a sigh, "is what I read in the newspaper."

Lonnie Zamora was born in Magdalena, New Mexico, on September 7, 1933. His father, Domingo, was a cement plasterer. The youngest of nine children, Zamora was thirteen when Domingo died. His mother, Rafelita, moved the family first to Morenci, Arizona, then later to Socorro.

From the time he was young, Zamora has always known hard work. When his mother died while he was still a teen-ager, Zamora quit high school and took a job in construction. Later, after marrying Mary and becoming the father of two children, he took any job he could. He worked at New Mexico Tech in maintenance. He was a bailiff for a local judge. A long-time ambition was to become a New Mexico state policeman. A lack of education prevented him from making it. Instead, Zamora went to work for the Socorro Police Department. By all accounts he was a competent officer. He was considered conscientious and trustworthy. Zamora had been with the police department for five years when he went to the arroyo.

Being a small-town lawman did not prepare Zamora for instant celebrity status, and he has trouble coping with it still. After strangers showed up on Zamora's doorstep without an appointment and ordered him to take them to the arroyo, he grew irritated. When pests insisted Zamora accept long-distance telephone calls—collect calls, often—he became bugged. Of the hundreds of letters Zamora has received, he has only answered a handful. He grew weary of defending himself long ago.

From the outset, Zamora decided to cooperate with only those people he trusted, such as Hynek, who became his friend. The two men kept in touch. The famed astronomer would occasionally ask Zamora to join him at speaking engagements. Zamora respectfully declined. "I ain't no speaker," he says. Zamora turned down an invitation in 1970 to be flown to Mexico to meet with a group of individuals who all claimed to have sighted UFOs. "They wanted me to join their club," Zamora says. "I ain't no joiner."

Money, even in the form of airline tickets to Mexico, has never interested Zamora. He says a writer from a flashy supermarket tabloid once descended on his Socorro house with an offer. The writer was willing to hand over $100 if Zamora would change his story and spice it to suit the tabloid's readers: "Cop Beams Up to Make Alien Bust." Zamora closed his door in the writer's face.

Zamora left the Socorro Police Department six years after the incident. For a while he ran a Chevron station on N.M. 60, on the western edge of Socorro. In the mid-1970s he again became a city employee when he joined the maintenance department. Today he drives an earth mover. He supplements his income by serving in the National Guard. A lesser man might have turned to drink after going through what Zamora did. Zamora turned to work and, he says, to God. His mother gave him his religious faith. "I pray every day," says Zamora. "I couldn't have gotten through this without God's help." He says he doesn't think much about the event unless someone brings it up. He has been back, but not lately, to the lonely arroyo, located just west of where a KOA campground now stands. He doesn't like to go there, he says. He would rather be at home where he enjoys watching television. "Hee-Haw" is his favorite program. No, he has not seen *E.T.* or *Close Encounters of the Third Kind*. He does not go to the movies. "My husband is a simple man but a good one," says Mary Zamora. "He wouldn't talk about this, but he is kind-hearted. When he was a policeman, he was always helping out vagrants, you know, people stranded. When he owned the service station, he did the same thing: took money out of his own pocket to give to somebody who was in trouble."

The U.S. Air Force's official report on the Socorro incident is inconclusive. Twenty years later, Zamora's sighting is still on the unexplained list of Project Blue Book at Wright-Patterson Air Force Base in Ohio. Project Blue Book is the bible of data taken from all reported UFO phenomena. The Air Force's findings, or lack thereof, do leave little questions unanswered. A few minutes before Zamora's sighting, someone telephoned an Albuquerque television station to report a UFO was "heading south of the city." There were no reports on radar screens on the early evening of April 24, 1964, but the screens at White Sands and Holloman Air Force Base terminated at 5:00 P.M. After the object allegedly landed and then took off from the arroyo, a crystalline-like substance formed on the greasewood bush that had been seared. Those people around Socorro familiar with the area's plant life could not explain the substance. Neither could the Air Force.

Most people who have studied the case in depth truly believe Zamora saw something. James Luckie feels it was an American spacecraft. "Ithat outfit we went to the moon on. It come up from Alamogordo. The reason I know this is that when I got out there I smelled diesel fuel. I know that smell 'cause I worked on highways for twenty-five years. And what UFO uses diesel fuel?"

Zamora says that at first he thought it was some kind of Air Force plane because the Air Force investigators took charge of everything. "They were really busy here for a while." He also figured it belonged to the government because of the inverted red *V* he saw on the side of the craft, an insignia that has never been figured out. Now Zamora isn't sure of anything except this: he was at the wrong place at the wrong time. "If something like this should ever happen to me again, if I should ever see anything strange out there, I know what I'll do," says Zamora, stroking his big knuckles. "I won't tell nobody."

II

Trails

Waterway

From the road, it often appears as a green tunnel. From the air, it is a white snake asleep in the sun. Up close, it is liver-brown in certain places, gullet-gray in others. The Rio Grande or, as it's known in some circles of geographic redundancies, the Rio Grande River, travels 450 miles in New Mexico. With more than half the state's population living near it, the river knows death and life: it has served as a depository for murder weapons and as a font for baptisms. It has been flooded and, to borrow from Will Rogers, been in need of irrigation. Said one pithy observer: "Too thick to drink, too thin to plow."

Any one who attempts to explore the Rio Grande—and to record what he sees—must do so in the overwhelming shadow of New Mexico's man of belles lettres, Paul Horgan. Horgan spent fourteen years learning about this river. To research his monumental, Pulitzer Prize-winning *Great River*, published in 1954, Horgan examined the Rio Grande, from its source in Colorado to its mouth in the Gulf of Mexico, by car three times. He parked along river roads, took notes, and made field sketches while the motor ran. Horgan once told me that originally he wanted to journey the Rio Grande by helicopter. He would pen a long piece about it for *Life* magazine, and his old friend, artist Peter Hurd, would contribute drawings. But the chopper never got off the ground. Sikorsky Aircraft, which Horgan hoped to persuade to lend him a helicopter gratis, literally told the writer to take a hike.

My plan wasn't to buzz the river, or even to make poetry of it, as Paul Horgan did. I wanted to follow it. Like Spanish explorers of 400 years ago, my river course would be south to north. Unlike some conquistadors, however, I would not be hunting gold. I would be looking for people with stories to tell, stories about the river.

It is mid-morning and ninety-four degrees upriver from El Paso, Texas, near the New Mexico border. The Rio Grande here produces the sticky smell of overripe bananas. Alongside me is John Montoya, a thirty-three-year-old U.S. border patrolman. In front of us is "the Line," Border Patrol talk for the Rio Grande. The Line is the chief point over which illegal aliens enter New Mexico.

The muddy water in the river this day is thigh-high. Illegals can walk across. A few weeks before, when the river was deeper, Montoya nabbed a woman being ferried over on the shoulders of a male friend.

John Montoya has been working the Line for six years. He is a square-shouldered, no-nonsense type. Strapped to his hip is a .357 Magnum. He has never used the gun. "There's little violence in this business," Montoya says. "Mostly it's just catching them [illegals] and sending them back without criminal charges." The Border Patrol catches about one out of three illegals on the Line. In 1981, 149,000 were apprehended. I ask Montoya if the numbers depress him. "It's aggravating," he responds. "You know you can't get them all. You do the best job you can."

Surprisingly, most illegals come across the river during daylight hours. Some hold dry clothing over their heads. Others carry chisels to tear holes in the controversial "Tortilla Curtain," a seven-mile protective fence that runs along the river in El Paso.

This morning, a half-dozen restless males are seated in plain sight on the Mexican side. A staring contest is broken only by jeers. "Aguacate!" the Mexicans yell. The word is Spanish for "avocado," the color of Montoya's uniform. Montoya has caught illegals as young as three and as old as eighty. Most try to cross in groups, and most give variations of the same story: that they have a sick relative in the States. Only once has Montoya believed this story. When he checked he found an alien's wife was indeed ill in a Chicago hospital. Four years ago Montoya observed a Ford Bronco stuck in the middle of the Line. When the border patrolman went over to the car, its passengers fled. Inside, Montoya found 514 pounds of marijuana.

Montoya grew up in Albuquerque. As a child he picnicked along the Rio Grande with his parents, and took occasional raft trips on the river. Now he guards it for $22,500 a year. "The challenge of this job is to enforce the law," he tells me. The pleasures? "I'm outdoors and not behind a desk. Also, I like the people I meet." Suddenly, there is movement on the opposite bank. Montoya scans the border. "Aguacate!" comes a cry.

Thirty miles north of the Line sits Vado, a river town. *Vado* means "ford" in Spanish, and years ago this was the only place for miles where one could cross the Rio Grande. It's also one of the first all-black communities in New Mexico.

Hobart Boyer, an original Vado settler, came to the river seeking freedom. Grandson of a Georgia slave, Boyer arrived with other blacks in the mid-1920s. Cotton growers in the area were glad to see the newcomers. "They could hire us cheap," says Boyer with a laugh. He is a stout man with a prominent head and a jaw like a park bench.

Vado's blacks had the last laugh on the cotton growers. Land in the community was blanketed with irksome mesquite. The soil was alkali. Whites found the land hard to farm cotton on, so they started giving away plots to the blacks. On 2½ of those discarded acres Hobart and Bessie Boyer raised vegetables and children.

Vado has about 200 families. Approximately one-third now are white. Once the town had 2,000 residents and an all-black school. Discrimination kept Vado children out of other schools, including New Mexico A&M at Las Cruces.

Boyer will be eighty-two in December. Ill in recent years, he hardly ever goes to the river anymore. As a young man he used to go there with a 100-foot-long seine, a large, weighted fishing net. He would drop the seine into the river and pull out catfish by the score. "Can't do that no more," Boyer says, laughing again. "It's against the law. Just like slavery."

The Rio Grande sloshes along the western edge of Las Cruces. A century ago, before rechanneling, the river went through the heart of the city. In the basement of Jett Hall, on the campus of New Mexico State University, I stop to see Dr. John Minor, a professor of civil engineering. I have heard about a special club at NMSU that Minor advises. Each spring the club from State and one from the University of New Mexico face one another in competition on the Rio Grande. It is a regular college regatta, only the boats are made of concrete.

Minor reveals that the first year New Mexico State took part, the school's boat weighed nearly 700 pounds. "No one really understood what we were doing then. Myself included." That big barge did well in the races. Afterward, however, it was seen wallowing near the bottom of the Rio Grande, and was disqualified.

Concrete-canoe-racing rules state that if a boat fills with water, it must not sink. Student-builders are permitted to place Styrofoam in the concrete as a flotation aid. Yet to the unknowledgeable, the question still becomes, what keeps them up? Explains Minor, "Well, ships are made of steel, and steel weighs more than concrete. The key is the amount of water you displace as compared to the weight of the boat. It's a principle developed by Archimedes."

To the winning school goes a traveling trophy, a six-by-twelve-inch cylinder used to measure the strength of concrete. All schools must lug home their boats, but a new boat must be built each year. When competition is completed, team members and engineering students from both schools usually retreat to another body of liquid—a keg of beer.

NMSU usually hauls its used canoes to the dump or turns them into flower boxes. For the past few semesters, one end of the canoe has been cut off and mounted, deer head-style, on the wall of the student lounge. Following one race, the school unloaded its craft on the UNM campus. "It was the scroungiest-looking boat you ever saw," says Minor. "I'm sure UNM hated us for that. It probably wasn't the best way to cement relationships."

Gordon Solberg has never sat in a concrete canoe. He likes to refer to himself as a river dropout. Eight years ago, Solberg and his wife came to Radium Springs, seventeen miles north of Las Cruces. There on the Rio Grande they built a thriving ceramics business called Sun Mountain Arts. With four employees helping, the Solbergs made decorative wall displays—tomatoes for kitchens and choo-choo trains for children's bedrooms. Business boomed. Wholesalers coast to coast took on Sun Mountain's line. However, the task eventually became, in Solberg's words, "a drag and a hassle." Soon the Solbergs divorced, and Gordon's wife moved away. He was left with a studio filled with broken molds and a house without a toilet. At thirty-five, with only a herd of goats to keep him company, Solberg insists he's happy. "I could live on $1,000 a year now."

Solberg is a back-to-nature sort. He built his fifteen-room house single-handedly. He uses a windmill for water and raises grapes, asparagus, and honeybees. When he wants meat, he kills a goat. If there is a problem in this paradise it is mosquitoes. "They breed on this part of the river," Solberg says. "In the evening you can hear them whine. They move about in clouds."

Salt cedar certainly poses no problem. When Solberg moved in, his land was a jungle of salt cedar trees, as is much of the banks of the Rio Grande here. "Lots of people give a bad rap to salt cedar," says Solberg. "They say it robs you of irrigation and that it's useless. I feel otherwise. My goats love salt cedar leaves. And it makes excellent firewood. I've estimated that one-quarter of an acre of salt cedar will provide all the fuel a family will ever need."

Salt cedar has another use, according to Solberg. As prosperous as Sun Mountain Arts became, the firm never provided Solberg with enough time or money to install an indoor commode. He admits that is one reason his wife left. Yet Solberg swears his outhouse is quite civilized. "The wood ashes I put down there kills any odor right away." What kind of wood ashes? Salt cedar, of course.

It is difficult to follow the serpentine course of the Rio Grande through the Mesilla Valley and not stop at a farm. The one I select in the village of Rincon is a tidy and attractive 130 acres belonging to Nick and Rena Carson.

The sun is sagging when I pull in front of the Carsons' white-brick-with-Spanish-tile-roof farmhouse. Nick Carson and his three sons are out in the fields thinning chile. Rena is inside washing lettuce. The lettuce has a fresh look. Rena's face, sweat-streaked and tired, bears a scowl. "I been up since 3:00 A.M.," she grumps. "I'm cranky, so watch out."

Carson says she was awakened at three by a call from Caesario Martínez, the family's ditch rider. Martínez moves from farm to farm in Rincon, telling owners that the Rio Grande is ready to be sent through irrigation ditches.

There is not a farmer in the Mesilla Valley who isn't worried about the claims made during the early 1980s by Texas to water rights here. As much as this topic adds to Carson's crabbiness, it doesn't bug her half as much as the failure to get decent help. "Our family makes this farm go by working like dogs. Dogs, I tell you. The migrants around here go home on weekends. And they won't irrigate at night. The residents of this area aren't interested in the work."

Rena Carson grew up on a farm in nearby Salem. Her father taught her the virtues of backbreaking labor. "Work is all I've ever known.

When I was a little girl I never had time for pleasures, such as swimming. The river has got to be no taller than my knees for me to go in it. As much as we depend on water around here, I'm scared to death of the stuff."

Around the bend from Rincon are two little Sierra County villages known as Derry and Arrey. Straddling the Rio Grande, they are separated by a narrow steel bridge. Standing next to the Derry-Arrey span is a white clapboard home with a garden of red carnations out front. Elisha Edwin Moseley owns that house. When I ask him if he resides in Derry or Arrey, Moseley scratches his head. "For two years I got mail in Derry but I lived in Arrey. Now I get my mail in Arrey but suspect I live closer to Derry."

Dressed in bib overalls, Moseley is seventy-six. The Rio Grande has given him many stories—good, bad, and strange. Moseley homesteaded here on five acres in 1926. "At first I hauled all my drinking water right out of the river. It tasted great then, but I wouldn't put my tongue in it now." Life was pleasant in those early days. Moseley used to snare beaver here with a number four steel trap. He heard bullfrogs at night. Once he even caught an eel in the river.

In the 1940s, the International Boundary and Water Commission took over Moseley's waterfront. When the commission cut back the brush, the beaver disappeared. No eels were seen again. Moseley claims the commission paid him fifty dollars an acre when he had originally paid seventy-five. This bothers him still, especially at night when he lies in bed and can't hear the croak of a single frog.

Now for a strange story. Some years ago, when three adjacent Sierra County tributaries poured into the Rio Grande at a mighty rate, Elisha Edwin Moseley says he saw something he still can't believe. He says the force from that confluence actually, for a few brief moments, caused the river to run north.

Sitting in a fourteen-foot aluminum boat, fishing the south end of Caballo Reservoir, I think how fortunate I am to have such a grand companion in K. W. "Babe" Lanford. At Babe's feet rests a pile of white bass. On his mind dances a cold beer. Babe likes beer nearly as much as fishing. Beefy and instantly friendly, with the face of a walleyed pike, Babe has been fishing Caballo since before the Rio Grande was dammed up here in 1938 to make the lake. Babe thinks Caballo has the best fishing in New Mexico. He has reeled in a ninety-six-pound catfish to prove it.

Retired now, Babe fishes every day. When he's not on the lake he's in his trailer across from it, sipping Schlitz. But Babe doesn't drink and fish at the same time. "Too dangerous," he warns. "You wanna spill beer all over your boat?"

Babe knows all about accidents. For five years he ran the Caballo boat dock. For another five he patrolled the lake for the State Parks and Recreation Department. "Most of the folks I hauled out of here drowned because of carelessness. People don't respect the wind we got here. Or they'll git a little ol' boat and put six people in it and no safety equipment." Babe once witnessed a marriage on Caballo. Less than thirty minutes later he pulled the bride from the lake. She wasn't breathing.

Life on the water hasn't been all dark. Take the time Babe came upon a capsized catamaran. Sitting on the hull was the owner, soaked and angry. "I'd like to get that SOB," the man hollered to Babe, "who sold me this $10,000 boat and said it would never tip over." Then there was the fellow who saw on Caballo a floating log and swore to Babe it was the Loch Ness monster.

Babe and his wife reared two sons on Caballo. Both boys, not surprisingly, wound up in the Navy. One is in submarines, the other in underwater demolition.

Done fishing, we retreat to Babe's trailer. Wrapping his tan hands around the first of many Schlitzes, Babe drops a line. "There was this couple went out fishing one day. They see this ol' bachelor kind of lolling in a boat. He's too lazy to do anything but fish. The couple tells him he oughta get married and raise a family. The ol' boy looks up and says, real sleepy-like, 'You don't know any pregnant women, do you?' "

If Caballo Dam changed the shape of the Rio Grande, Elephant Butte Dam shaped changes in southern New Mexico. Elephant Butte Dam took six years to build. It was completed in 1916 and supplies electric power for the Mesilla Valley and beyond. At the time it was constructed, the dam was the largest slab of concrete in the United States. The Bureau of Reclamation ramrodded the project. Superintendent of construction was Robley J. Schmalhausen. His daughter lives at Truth or Consequences, four miles south of the dam. "I'm not the oldest person in T or C," says Sophie Hedrick, a cheerful, septuagenarian history buff. "But I've lived here longest. There are very few people left who saw that dam go up."

During construction, Hedrick lived with 5,000 other families in the town of Elephant Butte. She remembers it as a sociable place with a hotel, movie theater, ice cream parlor, and tennis courts. Hot Springs, later T or C, barely existed then. Ironically, while T or C has grown into a prosperous community, Elephant Butte has shrunk to almost nothing. All that's left of the community are the stone foundations of old houses and the town jail. The houses were for higher-echelon construction families like the Schmalhausens. Other people lived in tents.

When the dam was finished, the Schmalhausens moved to Mexico, then to El Paso, Texas, where Robley took jobs. Fifty years ago he returned to gaze upon what man had wrought from the Rio Grande. He was killed when his car went off the road at Elephant Butte.

Sophie Hedrick's T or C home is located, appropriately, on Riverside Drive. The Rio Grande lies thirty yards from her dining room window. Here the water is emerald-colored and invigoratingly cold. "It's just come out of Elephant Butte Lake," Hedrick explains as I pull my arm from the river. Hedrick reveals a secret: the dam was surveyed by one B. M. Hall. "At first they were going to call it B. M. Hall Lake," she whispers. "Later they changed their minds." I tell her that I think they made the right choice. She nods.

Floods have broken the Rio Grande in New Mexico several times since man began keeping records. Notable overflows occurred in 1903, 1911, 1913, 1920, 1935, and 1941. Perhaps the most famous flood took place in late summer of 1929. It inundated an area below Socorro, and caused the flourishing town of San Marcial to vanish. That's a story that has been told before. Other, lesser-known towns were hit by the '29 flood. One was tiny Luis Lopez, six miles south of Socorro. There's little chance of flooding here now. The strength of the Rio Grande at Luis Lopez has been cut into three bodies of water: river, canal, and drainage ditch.

Waiting for me near the center of Luis Lopez, relocated since the Great Flood, is Flora Montoya, stern-faced and taupe-haired. Born in 1910, Montoya was reared here, as were her father and grandfather. As a child she used to cross the river on a horse and buggy to visit her grandfather's ranch in the bosque. If the water was deep enough, Santiago Padilla liked to give his granddaughter rides on a homemade pole boat.

Montoya was attending school in Socorro when the Great Flood struck. She stayed put. Her sister was teaching school south of Luis Lopez. She almost died. "My father went to rescue her. When he got there, my sister was standing on a hill. Everything else was underwater."

For several years, Montoya and her husband, Hino, operated the Green Valley Grocery in Luis Lopez. The store has been closed since 1950. Now the Montoyas farm hay and visit their grandchildren. Nobody knows what happened to the pole boat.

A telephone call interrupts our conversation. After speaking to a friend in Socorro, Montoya returns with a stricken look. It isn't the river that has her troubled this time. "In Socorro this morning," she says, her face pale, "something bad happened. There was an earthquake."

Unlike Las Cruces, Albuquerque has the Rio Grande flowing through its core. Author Paul Horgan, who grew up in New Mexico's largest city, used the river as a playground as a boy. "It was always warm and brown and voluptuous. I loved to roll in it." The river in Albuquerque is part of the city, in terrain and in name. The Albuquerque telephone directory shows more than forty listings for organizations with the words Rio Grande in their names—from Rio Grande Amusements to the Rio Grande Zoological Park. Because the river plays such a large role in the life of the city, tragedy more than occasionally appears within its waters. Since 1959, more than 125 people have drowned in Middle Rio Grande Conservancy District ditches, the chain of spillways that flow from the river in Bernalillo County.

Mike and Dolores Garcia live just east of Albuquerque's Coors Road, about a mile from the Rio Grande. The Garcias' only son used to walk to the river regularly. "Gene liked to collect snakes and bring them home," his mother recalls. "Once he brought the branch from a Russian olive he'd found on the riverbank." "He planted it in our front yard," offers Mike Garcia. "The tree's growing real well."

Despite her son's discoveries, Dolores Garcia used to plead with Gene to stay away from the river. "Don't worry, Mom," he'd tell her. "I'll be okay." One Saturday morning in May 1979, fifteen-year-old Gene and two friends went to a stretch of the Rio Grande, between Interstate 40 and Central Avenue, called Cocoa Beach. There the river widens into the Arenal Canal. Warm weather and an orange-crate raft beckoned the trio into the water. One of the youths slipped. Reaching to grab him, Gene fell in and disappeared into a whirlpool later estimated to be thirty feet deep.

For eighteen days police scuba divers, neighborhood friends, and the Garcia family searched for the youth. Mike Garcia told his employer he would not return to work until his son was found. For sixteen hours each day, Garcia combed the mucky, insect-plagued shoreline. He found many things: fifteen shopping carts, ten patches of quicksand, rats as big as cats, a fifty-pound pig, a kitchen sink even. But not Gene.

"We didn't give up hope," says Mrs. Garcia. "There was always the chance Gene had hit his head and crawled out of the river with amnesia. We had to keep the faith." Mrs. Garcia knew, however, how ruthless the river could be. Years before, her father and uncle were riding in a pickup that went off a Belen bridge. Her uncle was thrown clear and lived. Pinned in the truck, her father drowned in the Rio Grande.

A ditch cleaner at Isleta Bridge, seventeen miles south of Cocoa Beach, spotted Gene's body. Mike Garcia took the loss extremely hard. "It's like part of you is gone," he says softly. "We were so close. Before Gene died I was happy-go-lucky. For a long time after I was short-tempered. It's still very hard for me to see other men with their sons." The Garcias say even driving over a Rio Grande bridge is difficult for them now. The couple's two other children, Pauline, seventeen, and Michelle, sixteen, are not allowed near the water. "Given a chance," says Mike Garcia, running a hand over his thinning hair, "that river will take you."

Tragedy reappears by the time I arrive at San Felipe Pueblo and Frank Tenorio's home. Four days earlier, a twelve-year-old San Felipe boy had been swimming in the Rio Grande. Someone from the pueblo has found his body this afternoon. Saddened as Frank Tenorio is by the death, he nevertheless agrees to a visit. Tenorio was born at San Felipe sixty years ago. His roots go deep into the 700-year-old pueblo, and the cool *cheena* that flows past it. "I have a healthy respect for the Rio Grande," Tenorio says, settling his large frame into a living room sofa. "The river is a spirit. We Indians talk to it, revere it like Catholics pray to saints. The river cleanses our attitudes, our thoughts, even our souls."

As a former governor of San Felipe, Tenorio chooses his words carefully. "The river is religious, but if I say too much about it the pueblo elders will crucify me." What he does say is that San Felipeans, like all Pueblo Indians, worship natural things. Their worshipping is undermined when people—white people in particular—tinker with nature. Cochiti Dam sits just up the Rio Grande from San Felipe. As beneficial as that dam seems, Tenorio feels it is a prime example of white people tinkering with—and destroying—something natural.

Tenorio claims there is algae in the river now, thanks to the dam. When the river was wild, before Cochiti Dam was built, Tenorio says he can remember beautiful crushed ice floating by during winter. No more. He says on warm days he used to see soft-shell turtles on the banks. No longer. In place of the ice and turtles are large deposits of eroding silt, a menace the pueblo must rid itself of annually.

Still, the river has been good to San Felipe. The pueblo is just now enjoying a rebirth of agriculture, after years of dormancy. And while the Rio Grande reaches one of its narrowest points in New Mexico at San Felipe, there has never been a flood here. "I guess," reckons Tenorio, "that the spirits are with us."

Although the Rio Grande passes twenty miles west of Santa Fe, the river may one day hold great significance for New Mexico's second largest city. In 1984, Santa Fe officials made plans to import water from the river in case of an emergency. It won't be cheap—as few things in Santa Fe are. It costs about thirty-five cents per thousand gallons to deliver Santa Fe water to area users. It would cost about one dollar and fifteen cents more to deliver the same amount of Rio Grande water to the Santa Fe area.

Twenty miles northeast of Cochiti Lake, the Rio Grande runs by another pueblo, San Ildelfonso. Here, a spot called Otowi Bridge forms the setting for one of the most beloved books about New Mexico. *The House at Otowi Bridge* (pronounced *Oh-ta-wee*) first appeared in 1959. Peggy Pond Church, the book's author, had only meant her work to serve as a little tribute to its subject, Edith Warner. A spinster who lived in a simple shack in remote Otowi, Edith Warner for more than twenty years watched the river and life roll by. The book's charming, wistful quality caught on with readers. Still in print, *The House at Otowi Bridge* is one of the most successful titles the University of New Mexico Press ever put forth. Through five paperback printings and several in cloth, the book has become a southwestern classic.

Edith Warner died in 1952. Peggy Pond Church is nearly eighty, but remarkably chipper. In fact, this morning she agrees to accompany me on a picnic to Otowi Bridge. Church supplies the food: cold turkey breast sandwiches and dry sherry.

Before our meeting I reread Church's book. Edith Warner was a young woman when she left Pennsylvania for New Mexico in the 1920s. Her first job was to check freight unloaded by a narrow-gauge railroad that ran beside the one-lane suspension bridge at Otowi. Eventually, Warner opened a tearoom there. It became "The House by the Side of the Road." During World War II, scientists working on the Manhattan Project at Los Alamos, such as J. Robert Oppenheimer and Niels Bohr, used to while away the hours in Warner's little adobe. From these events Peggy Pond Church wove a non-fiction account of a shy, frail woman who lived and died, as San Ildefonso Indians put it, "where the water makes a noise."

Edith Warner's Otowi Bridge home has been gone for years. This gladdens Church. "If they had made it into a literary shrine," she says, pouring sherry, "I think that would have been fatal." One Hollywood scenarist wanted to pen a script of the Otowi book, but Church refused. "They were going to turn Edith's life into a romance, fictionalize it. Not in my lifetime." Recently, however, following a small but highly complimentary piece about the book in the *New York Times*, UNM Press received several serious queries regarding movie rights.

Otowi Bridge still sways in the wind, but it cannot be traversed. A larger steel span takes travelers up to Los Alamos, the town where Church went to live when she was twenty. Beneath both bridges the river does make a noise. Edith Warner called the sound "the melody of living." "Edith was a very private person," Church says, gathering her picnic goods. "She liked to live along this river and not go anywhere. She always felt there was something magical about the Rio Grande. She said if you put your finger in the river and asked a question, you'd get an answer."

Many people ask this question of Española: why does it get picked on so much? Española, through which the Rio Grande cuts a shiny, doeskin swath, is like Rodney Dangerfield: it gets no respect. Española has, in fact, turned into a Hispanic Clines Corners. No one is sure why the community, with a population of 8,900, has become the focus of so many cruel jokes. It just is. Some samples: Do you know why the Española Public Library had to close? Someone checked out the only book. Did you hear about the hurricane that hit Española? It did two million dollars in improvements.

The barbs bother some people, but most residents have come to accept the slights. "They're just Polish jokes with Española inserted," says Judy Vigil, of the Española Valley Chamber of Commerce.

"It's good for business. I don't think there's anything wrong with laughing at yourself."

There is a serious side to Española and I discover a piece of it on a bridge that steps over the Rio Grande. A plaque on the trestle indicates the structure is named for Phil Isidore Valdez, an Española native who died while serving as a Navy medic in Vietnam. Valdez's age strikes me as the cruelest joke of all. When he was killed in action near Da Nang he was only twenty.

Standing on a shoreline in the village of Embudo, I find myself staring at an empty oxygen tank hanging from a tree. Some youths tell me to hit the tank with a stick, which I do. *Cluuuunnnng! Cluuuunnnng!* The noise brings a young man in blue bathing trunks to the opposite bank. He climbs on a wooden platform and then glides across the river—about 180 feet—on a pulley-driven trolley. Arriving on my side, the young man introduces himself as Roger Pettit. He explains he is the caretaker for a cabin on the other side of the Rio Grande. The only way to get to that cabin, he says, is by the trolley.

The cabin's owner, Tom Watson, desires privacy. Watson is an inventor who lives in Santa Fe. Wishing to flee city life on weekends, Watson, some years ago, came to out-of-the-way Embudo and strung his cable. "Mr. Watson is just about the most marvelous man I ever met," says Pettit. "You know those old clothes dryers? Well, Mr. Watson turned one into a composter. And he's going to take parachutes and rope and harness them to the river so's we'll have electricity in the cabin."

Roger Pettit hails from near Lubbock, Texas. A year ago he was bumming around the West. He planned to settle eventually in the Canadian wilderness. Stopping in Embudo, north of Española, he met Tom Watson and was offered a job. Pettit calls the job "the dream of a lifetime."

When Watson shows up he parks his car beneath the oxygen tank doorbell, fills the trolley with food, and pulleys himself across the river. "You wouldn't ever want to try to drive a car across here," Pettit warns me. "It's about six feet deep here and the current, a real killer certain times, is seven or eight miles an hour." When the river was lower, Pettit says his boss drove an old school bus across. It serves now as the cabin's kitchen. A bus for a kitchen? Yessir, boasts Pettit. "Mr. Watson is just about the smartest man I ever met. I'm getting so much experience being around him. When I go up to Canada,

I'll know a lot more than I ever would. I got it all right on this here river."

The best (and some people believe only) way to appreciate the upper Rio Grande is by holding on (some people say for dear life) to a raft. Ron Van Nevel is a chunky ex-schoolteacher from Chicago. He is also a confirmed river rat. Van Nevel is co-owner of Taos's Sierra Outfitters and Guides, one of the oldest and largest whitewater rafting enterprises on the Rio Grande.

The code word, or rather code initials, for Van Nevel and just about everyone else who works the river in these parts, is "cfs." That's cubic feet per second, or the amount of water flowing past any given point at any given time. "We've got about 2,000 cfs on the river right now," Van Nevel tells me at his Taos office. "The Bureau of Land Management won't let us raft below 900."

The following day, with the river at 1,910 cfs, I join Van Nevel in an eighteen-foot gray rubber bathtub. At Arroyo Hondo we begin a seventeen-mile course that will finish at Taos Junction. A thermometer in the raft shows the water to be an icy forty-three degrees. Rafting with me is a group of emergency-room workers from an Albuquerque hospital. They are a quick-witted bunch. "If you fall in and swallow water," one advises, "spit it out."

Van Nevel serves as our boatman. His job is to steer us around rocks and over waves in one piece. His ad hoc role is to make constant references to food consumption. For instance, Van Nevel is extremely conscious of safety precautions: he has little tolerance for those who aren't. "You fall in at certain places on this river," he cautions, "you'll eat your lunch." Those certain places in the rapids are known as holes. According to Van Nevel, should you drop in one, you'll "eat" the hole. Here's Van Nevel on an especially bad spill: "I can't believe he ate the hole thing." North of Questa to the Colorado border are sections of the Rio Grande that rafters and anyone else should avoid. Not only will you eat your lunch there, Van Nevel promises, but you'll probably never eat again.

Awesomely beautiful as the Rio Grande is around Taos, Van Nevel doesn't fail to omit any menu items, no matter how gruesome: an Air Force pilot once struck a power line over the famed Rio Grande Gorge. He scattered his craft—and himself—for two miles. A kayaker hit a hole and had his life jacket sucked off. His body was found at Elephant Butte. A canoeist fell overboard and disappeared. A year later the man's tennis shoe was spotted. Inside was a foot.

Hearing such stories it's little wonder that when Van Nevel announces a for-real lunch stop, some rafters (me, especially) aren't terribly hungry.

A final and less grim note on rafting the Rio Grande: it is statistically safer than driving a car.

It is difficult to travel the Rio Grande and see everything. I never witnessed, for example, anyone being sold down the river, or up. Nor did I notice anyone swapping horses in midstream, or even by the shore. What I did see were people—the soul of the river. It is people like Elisha Edwin Moseley and Frank Tenorio and Flora Montoya who make the Rio Grande what it is: a timeless, living pathway, sometimes filled with water, always lined with stories.

Backbone

Some motorists swear crossing it causes their sinuses suddenly to drain like a colander. Other people, mostly Yankees, have been known to imagine it as a gargantuan wall or a petrifyingly deep chasm. On a road map it often appears as a dribble of dots or dashes, or a series of pup tents, one pitched upon another.

Like the International Dateline or the Tropic of Cancer, the Continental Divide is one of those boundaries that, though familiar, is sometimes misunderstood, even to the point of absurdity. *Question*: When did Congress authorize construction of the Continental Divide? *Answer*: Around the same time it passed the law of gravity.

First, it's not the Continental Shelf, which has to do with the ocean bottoms nor Continental Drift, which has to do with, well, drifting. Nor does it have any connection with the John Belushi movie, *Continental Divide*. That film had about as much to do with the Continental Divide as the moon has to do with moonshine.

Simply, a continental divide is an elevation of land that pushes water to opposite sides of a continent. In North America, where it is often called "the Backbone," the Divide usually is a bumpy ridge that sends eastward-flowing rivers to the Atlantic Ocean and westward-flowing ones to the Pacific. The Backbone meanders 3,100 miles through five states: New Mexico, Colorado, Wyoming, Idaho, and

Montana. Generally, it follows mountain ranges, particularly the Rockies. In New Mexico, it doesn't follow mountains. In fact, the Continental Divide, which saws through nine western New Mexico counties, courses this state as it does no other. In many places in New Mexico, the Great Divide, as it's also called, is barely distinguishable.

The Divide's origin in southern New Mexico is a jagged rock outcropping alongside Cloverdale, a crumb on the desert tableland. After wiggle-waggling its way north for 790 miles, the hogback slips into Colorado just north of Lumberton. Hikers have been known to travel the Continental Divide from Mexico to Canada. But it is not a trip for the faint-hearted: fewer than ten backpackers a year make the total journey. In many places the trek turns so remote that one hiker, fearing he might become lost, carried an aircraft-locater beacon. Though the U.S. Forest Service is studying ways to carve a trail along the Continental Divide, that path, which must periodically pierce private land, is not yet designated and may never be completely marked. Obstacles abound. On the Jicarilla Apache Reservation in northern New Mexico, for example, the government set up a Continental Divide Trail Committee. After several meetings the committee, which was interested in promoting tourism in the area, decided the trail should not cross the reservation.

Recently, I traveled the length of the Divide in New Mexico. I went on the trail and off it. I went by car, foot, and horse and, quite often, by instinct. In scratching the Backbone, I found what makes the Great Divide significant in New Mexico: it is rich in human experiences. In other states the Divide goes mostly into wilderness areas where few humans dwell. In New Mexico, however, it snakes through back yards, volcanoes, copper mines, a shopping mall, and people's lives.

I am standing on the bottom of what is called New Mexico's boot heel. If the Tony Lama Company were to nail taps on this heel, the metal would be right on top of me. When the Continental Divide enters the United States, its first thirty miles rip directly up the middle of the Gray Ranch, near Cloverdale. It's hard to stand anywhere in the boot heel of New Mexico without touching the Gray. At 500 square miles, almost half the size of Rhode Island, the Gray is the largest spread in southwestern New Mexico. There are sixty-eight windmills on the ranch. In front of me is one of the largest men in southwestern New Mexico, a man nearly as big as a windmill. Lonnie Moore is boss man of the Gray.

"The Divide makes this ranch," Moore says as he saddles what seems to be the largest horse in the corral. "The Divide acts as a watershed for us. Without water down here, we're stuck, like a Christmas pig." With a succinct manner and dead-ahead stare, Lonnie Moore is all cowboy. Only his baby-blue neckerchief looks out of character. Moore says the Gray was named for a homesteader who arrived here a century ago. Now the ranch is owned by a Los Angeles corporation with the unwestern title of American Breco.

I have arrived at the Gray during roundup, the busiest time of the year. During roundup, Moore pushes the ranch's eleven permanent hands to work "six-a-weeks." "Cowboyin's not the same as it once was," says Moore, as if working six days a week from first light to last isn't enough. Moore grew up in Duncan, Arizona. At age forty-seven, he has been riding the Gray for sixteen years. During that time Moore has seen several strangers cross the ranch, on the way up the Continental Divide Trail. When Moore spots a stranger, he escorts him off. Just as no one quibbles with a Brahman bull, no one argues with Lonnie Moore. "This is private property," he emphasizes bluntly. "It's all deeded land."

Moore prefers horseback himself, even when going to the top of Animas Peak, an 8,500-foot landmark located at the center of the Gray. "That hiking the Divide stuff, it don't go for me."

If Lonnie Moore seems to come from central casting, Steve Dobrott does not. He is dressed in chaps but wears wire-rimmed glasses. He looks like a college student, and, in fact, a few years ago he was. Dobrott is the Gray Ranch's wildlife biologist. But come roundup time, Dobrott, like everyone else on the Gray, pulls six-a-weeks. "I've been here five years," he says. "I could be here another five, and they'd still call me 'dude.'" When the dude isn't herding cattle, one of his jobs is checking both sides of the Divide for endangered species. Dobrott says there are about twelve in the area, from Mexican pronghorn antelope to the ridgenosed rattlesnake. "What does a ridgenosed rattlesnake look like?" Dobrott repeats the question, then pauses to wipe his spectacles. "It's a small snake, about eighteen inches. If you're looking for one, you'll probably never see it. If you aren't, you just might."

Up the way from the Gray, in the town of Animas, there are no rattlers and hardly anything else. *Animas* means "departed souls" in Spanish, and that is just what happened to a roadside cafe here. The cafe displays a curious sign and name. The sign features a cowboy and the greeting "aloha." The name is Willie Upshaw's Nightmare. Inside, the place is empty. However, it once was the only spot in Animas for young people to gather. The cafe became so crowded with teen-agers who cut school to play Asteroids and drink orange slushes that the owner, Upshaw, dubbed his establishment the Nightmare. Animas school officials grew to dislike Willie Upshaw's Nightmare. Officials finally said any youngster who wanted to frequent the Nightmare must have a note from his parents. That's why the Nightmare now is a very sleepy place.

Having always wanted to see a company town, I turn off at Playas, on the eastern slope of the Divide. A sort of Levittown in the desert, Playas was built by the mining conglomerate, Phelps Dodge. The town's 265 nearly identical three-bedroom house poke out of the parched earth like baked corn muffins. Eleven miles down the Divide lies the reason for those houses: the Phelps Dodge copper smelter. If you live in Playas, I discover, you work at the smelter.

Bob Napper, a sturdy, tanned man in his fifties, shuts off his lawn mower to talk. Napper has been working for Phelps Dodge for more than twenty years. He has lived in Playas since the town opened in 1975. Pushing back a brown ball cap and wiping his brow, Napper says that a good introduction to Playas is through terminology. As befits something new, something bursting with prefabricated efficiency, Playas is wealthy in abbreviations and nicknames. Rarely is Phelps Dodge referred to as anything other than the initials "P. D." "P. D." goes the oft-heard remark, "treats you well." In the same manner, those who live in Playas hardly ever call their community Playas. Instead, they say "townsite." "If you live in the townsite," says Napper, "P. D. will fix your house anytime something goes wrong."

Offering me lemonade, Napper says that much of life in Playas revolves around the Phelps Dodge Mercantile, the company store. "The store" is the only spot for miles where one can buy food, where one can buy anything. The store sells everything from washing machines to jewelry to shotguns. Napper goes to the store on his work holidays, which are called "off days." Like most smelter employees, he works twelve consecutive days before getting two off-days. The best day of all, says Napper, draining his drink, is every other Friday. That's payday.

As pleasant as life might appear in Playas, paydays have been coming with less frequency for some P. D. employees. In fact, Bob Napper is afraid: the copper industry is suffering. Low prices and government-subsidized foreign competition have severely cut into the smelter's output. P. D. has begun laying off people. "Everybody in the townsite," says Napper, returning to his yard work, "is praying real hard this thing will turn around soon."

Geographers call the region where the boot heel of New Mexico pokes out the Lower Sonoran Zone. Plant life thrives here. Yuccas often reach the height of a basketball rim. Chamisa sprouts fist-size flowers. Back across the Divide and north of Animas is a valley that annually looks as if it has been covered by a white bedspread. There are other places in New Mexico where cotton is grown, but there's only one Cotton City.

Of the 180 people in Cotton City, about fifty farm cotton. Like cattle at the Gray Ranch, cotton in Cotton City is gathered in the fall. Groundup time, you might call it. The harvest crop is brought to the place that keeps Cotton City on the map: the Conejo Gin. Don Burton is part owner of the Conejo. The gin, explains Burton, an affable sort who wears sunglasses indoors, separates seed from lint. "We take out the trash," Burton says with a grin. The good stuff is sent to Deming. The trash goes elsewhere. One place it goes is into cooking oil.

Last year nearly 6,000 bales of cotton were ginned in Cotton City. Each bale weighed about 500 pounds, and each farmer received approximately eighty cents per pound. The cotton is soft in Cotton City, but the life is not. "Making money in this business," says Burton, "is like robbing the First National Bank. It's there, but you pay a heckuva price to get it."

From Cotton City, the Divide zigs east and then zags north toward Silver City. Just south of Silver City it plows straight through Tyrone, another Phelps Dodge company town, though much older than Playas. Here streets are named Bornite and Malachite and Azurite. The Divide in fact runs smack through Tyrone's reason for being: an open-pit copper mine. So huge is that hole that it is scooped with shovels the size of a Holiday Inn suite. But the scooping comes slow these days in Tyrone. Like Playas, its neighbor to the south, Tyrone has been hit by layoffs from the depressed copper industry that not even the mineral-rich Backbone may be able to save.

The tough times have united people in Tyrone. Curiously, however, up the road the Continental Divide has caused divisiveness. Congress recently appointed a committee to move the Divide. Yes, move it, as in jacking up an entire mountain range and carting it farther west. One proposed change would occur in Grant County. The move would reroute the Divide south from Reed's Peak through Cooke's Peak, then through the Florida Mountains, just east of Deming. Eventually, the Divide would leave the state near Columbus, instead of 100 miles west at Cloverdale, where it exits now.

Keith LeMay, chairman of the Grant County Tourism Promotion Committee, grimaces when I ask him about the move. "Silver City is the largest city adjacent to the Divide, from the Mexico border to Rawlins, Wyoming. We're an excellent stopover and supply point for hikers and horsemen who use the Continental Divide Trail. To move the Divide from here makes about as much sense as parking the Golden Gate Bridge in North Dakota."

Rufus and Rita Hotchkiss laugh out loud when I ask them about moving the Divide. From a front-room window in their 101-year-old brick house in Silver City, the Hotchkisses can see, on a clear day, parts of the Continental Divide. "They're gonna have to take our house with 'em," says Rufus, a gravelly voiced gent with a carefully scissored mustache. The Hotchkisses have lived on an eighty-acre farm in Silver City since 1947. They fell in love with the Divide long before that. Rita, gray-haired and direct, trains horses. "When you want to exercise an animal," she says, "just take him to a trail on the Continental Divide." Rufus is retired. "Wanna see the Divide up close?" he asks.

Riding shotgun, Rufus gives directions as I drive out of Silver City and north into the Gila National Forest. As we wind through Pinos Altos, a historic mining town perched atop the Divide, Rufus says he worked half his life as foreman of a Grant County copper mine. It was a job, he says, that gave him an interest in geology. "Not damn schoolbook geology, just common-sense stuff." The Continental Divide, adds Rufus, is 30 million years old, "give or take a century." Rufus says he wouldn't like to have been around when the Divide was formed. "There was this god-awful overthrust. A pooping up. You know, you take a box of crackers and put it on a car seat and then smack it in two. Half the crackers crumble one way and the other half the other." The rock in this part of the Continental Divide is igneous limestone, Rufus continues. The limestone is all the time causing "shakers," Rufus's word for landslides.

Upon reaching Signal Peak, Rufus decides we should leave our car and walk. "I know a lot of these trails," he says. "I cut them for the Forest Service. I do it for free. Nobody else wants to do it. I use a little, itty-bitty Remington chain saw on the overhead branches and an ax when things get thick." Rufus would like to see more people hike the Continental Divide Trail so the rest of the Gila trails won't look like third-hand carpet. But not enough people are aware of the trail, he says. "The thing about this Divide," explains Rufus, snapping a twig with his fingers, "is that you can be standing right on top of it and not even know it's there."

Raymond Schmidt always has known when the Divide was underfoot. For more than thirty years Schmidt searched from atop Lookout Mountain for fires in the Gila Wilderness. His post was a tower that stood on the Continental Divide. Now eighty-six, Schmidt lives near the Divide in a little ghost town with a name that sounds like a laundry detergent. Chloride, located northwest of Truth or Consequences in the Black Range, formerly was a rough-and-tumble mecca for silver mining. Today it has barely twenty-five people.

A slight man with a Vandyke beard, Raymond Schmidt looks more like a Bavarian watchmaker than the forest ranger and copper miner he once was. Schmidt sleeps in the kitchen of a two-room adobe in Chloride. He has lived in the town most of his life. "I went to the eighth grade here. Twice. I never cared much for reading." During World War I, Schmidt became a ranger on the Divide for the summer months. Come winter, he walked the Divide all the way to Tyrone, 130 miles. There he searched for copper.

If Schmidt had no yen for school, he did have a curiosity about life. In the 1930s he built a telescope by following instructions from an article in *Popular Mechanics*. Since then he has made three more telescopes, grinding some of the lenses himself. His twelve-inch model once was one of the biggest in New Mexico. These days, when nights are cloudless over the Divide, Schmidt walks out to a little wooden shed, unlocks a door and rolls back a tin roof. He sits behind a ten-inch, pale green telescope to peer at the Orion Nebula. On a blackboard in his observatory are rows of numbers. Schmidt never had much schooling but somehow he learned to compute astronomical distances. "It's not hard," he says with a shrug.

Though blessed with innate intelligence, Schmidt is stubborn. He still bathes in a tub in his kitchen. He collects rainwater in a barrel. The toilet paper in his outhouse is pages from an automobile accessories catalog.

Schmidt tells me his eyesight is not what it once was. His hearing is poor too, he says. But he claims his health is fine otherwise.

He sharpens saws for a living, and when a mining company wants someone to guide employees along the Divide, Schmidt volunteers. Every morning he mounts his Honda 70 trail bike and rides to Winston to get the mail. On special occasions Schmidt drives his other vehicle—a 1950 Studebaker coupe.

Several times recently Schmidt has run into a group he calls "hippie hoppies." Some wore beads around their necks and others wore earrings in their noses. Some wore nothing at all. They are the Rainbow Family. For a week this year the Rainbow Family has camped in Scales Canyon, hard by the Continental Divide, in an isolated pocket of the Gila Wilderness. The Rainbows like the Continental Divide. Four years ago they held their annual national gathering in Scales Canyon. Nearly 5,000 members turned out. This fall, during a special full moon observance, only 500 came. But it was enough to raise the eyebrows of several natives of the area. Says one native: "The only pot them Rainbows know is the kind they smoke."

The Divide weaves a crazy-quilt pattern through the Gila National Forest. An hour's drive from Raymond Schmidt's house rests the Rainbow Family retreat. When I enter their camp, a family member named Hawk greets me. Hawk is a thirty-one-year-old former mental health worker from southern California. He is wearing beads and a rumpled ski sweater. Hawk says the Rainbow Family has been in existence for twelve years. Most of the members are "road people." Anyone can join, Hawk says; there are no dues. "We're interested in harmony, peace, and freedom. Some people think we're a nudist colony. We're not. But no one here is embarrassed about taking off his clothes."

Another Rainbow, named Alan, wears his lush beard in braids. Alan once had homes in New York and Brazil. "My real home is with the Rainbows." Alan says that the heart of any Rainbow gathering is the council. It is a combination meeting, love-in, and group chant. "I've learned a lot at councils," Alan confesses. When pressed, he says, "I learned that you're strongest when you're the most naked."

Smokey, Robin, and their five-year-old daughter, Sylvan Dove, spent the Rainbow gathering in a tepee. When I stop by their tent I find them packing to go back to Madrid, New Mexico, where they make environmental sculpture. Do you like sleeping on the Continental Divide? I ask. Robin thinks for a moment, then answers in words that sound sprung from a Haight-Ashbury time warp. "This place is groovy," she gushes. "It's mellow. I give it a nine."

In terms of size, Catron County is the largest county in New Mexico. Although bigger than Connecticut, Catron has but one doctor. He is seventy-two years old, and he also serves as the veterinarian, dentist, pharmacist, and medical investigator. He rides a ten-speed bicycle and drives a twenty-five-year-old Cadillac. He practices acupuncture, utilizes hypnosis, fasts one day a week, and wears a toupee.

The Catron County seat is Reserve, a cattle-ranching and sawmill community a few miles west of the Divide. On a ridge overlooking the village sits a faded, one-story building. Inside is a scene out of Charles Dickens: chambers wind every which way; ceilings are high and dark; medical equipment is antiquated; the smell of antiseptic is strong. Standing in one doorway of Reserve's answer to the Old Curiosity Shop is Lloyd Galloway Foster, M.D. A slight, diffident man, he is wearing a flannel shirt, bola tie, dark trousers, and shoes discarded by a former nurse. Foster tells me that he was born in Clayton, New Mexico, grew up in Oklahoma, and studied medicine in Ohio. His specialty is proctology. "Course I don't get much chance to do that here anymore, except hemorrhoids once in a while. They say you can get those in New Mexico by sitting on cold rocks."

Foster came to New Mexico in 1936 to practice in the old mining town of Mogollon, twenty-two miles south of Reserve. Three years after the war ended he settled in Reserve. The roads that crisscross the Continental Divide in Catron County bring Foster most of his patients. These roads feature hairpin turns, tiny shoulders, and frighteningly steep embankments. During his forty years in the area, Foster has seen many cars take the plunge. "Mess ups," he calls the auto accidents. Though an extremely gentle man, a pillar of the local Baptist Church, Foster frequently talks of his work in a ghoulish fashion. For instance: "One time, a huge pile of lumber toppled over on this Forest Service fella near the Continental Divide. He wasn't any thicker than this [holds his fingers a half-inch apart]. I mean, he was just pancaked, that guy was.

"A fella here, he was coming home from a prayer meeting when he dropped out of the back of a truck onto his head. I'm telling you, blood poured out of that boy's ear like a garden hose. You could hear it.

"One old gal, she went off the road in a mess-up on the Divide and dadgum if I didn't pull glass out of her face all one Sunday . . . tore half his scalp off . . . blew his leg away . . . fella just croaked."

Norma Foster, the physician's wife of twenty-two years, periodically acts as her husband's assistant. She is a small, gallant-looking woman who has been known to take a turn behind the wheel of the county ambulance. "Norma's done something I never did," says Foster, patting his hairpiece. "She pumped a stomach all by herself."

After a good run north of Reserve, the Continental Divide bites off a corner of the Ramah Navajo Indian Reservation before swallowing hunks of the Zuni Mountains. Just west of Grants, the Divide wraps itself around the rim of a volcanic crater called Bandera. Next door to Bandera are the Ice Caves. The Divide burrows through them, too. While the walls of Bandera are lavender in color, the walls of the Ice Caves are green. Algae green. The color quite possibly could make even Lloyd Foster ill.

The Continental Divide in the United States passes through twenty-five national forests and three national parks but only one town called Continental Divide. Located twenty-five miles east of Gallup, leaning on Interstate 40, Continental Divide might be termed Clines Corners West. The village, with a population of 200, is held together by four tourist shops. Gewgaws make up Continental Divide's stock in trade. On sale are cedar boxes stamped: "The more I see of some people the better I like my dog." There are plastic mugs stamped: "I want a perfect secretary—one who types fast and runs slow." There are pecan clusters, slingshots, and T-shirts stamped with the community's name, front and back. In fact, someone says if you stay in town long enough, you'll likely be tattooed "Continental Divide."

Claudell Hodges, a stately, proper woman, has been sorting mail in Continental Divide for fifteen years. She says it's a nice place to live, funny even. Tourists often drop by the post office to ask about the Divide. "Where's the big waterfall?" they ask. "You're standing on it," replies Hodges. Across Interstate 40 from the post office is a bar called Top of the World, in honor of the community's 7,275-foot elevation. The bar has a reputation for rowdiness. Last year two people died from injuries suffered at the Top of the World.

The grand potentate of the town of Continental Divide is probably Gene Gonzales. He runs one of the four tourist shops. A ringer for Paulie, the grizzled little butcher in all the *Rocky* movies, Gonzales has lived most of his life in Continental Divide. On a counter of his store is a dollar bill under glass. George Washington's face is not on the bill; Ronald Reagan's is. Yuk yuk. Gonzales's shop is shaped like an igloo. Gonzales says it was a real Navajo home at one time. "Know why Navajo husbands like round houses?" asks Gonzales, giggling at a joke he has probably told to 900 tourists. "Because their wives can never corner them." Yuk yuk.

One of the sparest regions of the Continental Divide is the leg that angles across the eastern half of McKinley County to Cuba, New Mexico. Perhaps more sheep than people populate this section. This stretch is not without color, however. Every month or so, when Navajo rugs are auctioned for thousands of dollars at Crownpoint, the landscape turns kaleidoscopic.

Northwest of Cuba, in little Lindrith, huddles the Trail's End Cafe. Spinning on one of the cafe's three stools is a man with a stomach that hangs over his belt like a Parma ham in a bag. His smile is a two-tooth salute. "Bill Chamblee's the name," the man booms at me, extending a hand the size of a dart board. When I ask Chamblee if he has been living in Lindrith long, he answers, "Oh, two or three days." Then he admits he came to Rio Arriba County in 1937 to farm and ranch. He is seventy-nine.

Chamblee tells me he is a staunch admirer of the weather along this western slope of the Divide. "You can breathe air that's not dirty, for one thing." He points out, however, that it can get cold in Lindrith. Flashing his two teeth—one goes north, he says, and the other one south—Chamblee reminisces: "I been here three times when the temperature's been fifty degrees below zero. I seen it so cold up on this Divide that little piñon bushes have plumb burned up." Chamblee and his wife, Mildred, have no children. But between them, the Chamblees have helped to rear many of the 125 people in Lindrith. In recognition of this fact, most of Lindrith is planning to attend the couple's fiftieth wedding anniversary. Chamblee says 400 people are coming. There will be 150 pounds of beef to eat. The reception will be held in Lindrith's American Legion Hall, and the dinner at the nearby office of the El Paso Natural Gas Company. "You're invited," Chamblee says, placing a huge paw on my shoulder. "Don't have to get all slicked up, neither. I'm not. Oh, I'll maybe put on a pair of clean Levi's."

The Continental Divide in Rio Arriba County twists back and forth across the Jicarilla Apache Indian Reservation, a course perhaps fifty miles in all. In Lumberton, just off the reservation, I decide to visit the C&C Trading Post. Two large, black Labradors, barking furiously, greet me in the driveway. "Don't worry," hollers a cheerful woman in a print blouse. "The dogs have already eaten this morning."

The woman is Verna Sherwood. She says she and her husband, Larry, are owners-operators of the C&C, which specializes in "junk and gifts." The junk is mainly rusted items like lawnmowers and dustpans. The gifts are what Larry creates: ducks, bells, lamps, toy cars, and roadrunner pinwheels. Larry Sherwood fashions these gizmos from dead aspen trees he finds along the Continental Divide. "Business is pretty good," reports Verna. What is there to do in Lumberton, I wonder. Verna, as if reading my mind, says, "You going to be here on Thursday night? If you are, there's bingo in the Catholic school gymnasium."

Back on the Jicarilla Reservation, oil and natural gas rigs stand posed along the Divide. To the Jicarillas, the striated, blood-red and plaster-white buttes of the Divide hold no particular spiritual significance. To white people, they hold wealth.

In Dulce, at the northern end of the reservation near the Colorado border, I meet a big, friendly Apache named Troy Vicenti. For years youngsters across the country devoured a comic strip called "Red Ryder and Little Beaver." Ryder was a fearless cowboy who did good deeds all over the West. Little Beaver was Ryder's faithful young Indian companion. The strip first appeared in 1938. At one time it was syndicated in 750 newspapers, including one I read as a boy. At one time, Troy Vicenti was little Beaver.

Fred Harman, a resident of Pagosa Springs, Colorado, just north of Dulce, created the comic strip. Every so often, when he needed a model for Little Beaver, Harman dropped in on the Jicarillas to look for one. In 1956, Harman spotted Vicenti and knew he had the perfect Little Beaver. The next 2½ years were, Vicenti tells me, the best years of his life.

Dressed in breechcloth and moccasins and packing a bow and arrow, Vicenti traveled the country with Fred Harman to promote the strip. Vicenti appeared on "Captain Kangaroo." He rode subways in New York City, he led parades in Los Angeles, California, he shook hands at rodeos in Dallas, Texas. "For an Indian from Dulce," says Vicenti, now thirty-five, "it was an incredible experience. I got to meet so many people, do so many things. I remember walking down Fifth Avenue in my costume and watching people clear out of the way." During public appearances, Vicenti got off his one great line, words anyone then in short pants knew by heart: "You betchum, Red Ryder." Vicenti does not know how many times he spoke that line. "Thousands, maybe."

When he wasn't promoting the strip, Vicenti lived on Fred Harman's ranch in Pagosa Springs. At night, Harman sketched the young-ster. During the day Vicenti rode Papoose, a pony that Harman owned. When he turned thirteen, Vicenti began to sit a little tall in the sad-dle. One day Harman broke the bad news: Vicenti was too big to be Little Beaver. It was a sad day, Vicenti says now. Then Vicenti smiles. Fred Harman, Vicenti recalls, could find no one to replace him. Want-ing to turn to fine art, the artist gave up the comic strip.

Vicenti kept in touch with Harman. When Vicenti joined the Marines and went to Vietnam, he received an encouraging letter from the artist. Later, people in Dulce started an event called the Little Beaver Roundup. (There already was a Red Ryder Roundup in Pagosa). Fred Harman eventually moved to Albuquerque and then, for health reasons, to Phoenix, Arizona. For several years Vicenti served as his reservation's guide for hunters and the Forest Service. As he rode and hiked the Continental Divide, Vicenti remembered the good times he had had with Harman, such as the time Little Beaver's black wig was knocked askew, or the day Harman gave Vicenti Papoose to keep.

In January 1982, Fred Harman died at age seventy-nine. Not long after, Troy Vicenti and three other men climbed on horses and rode deep into the high country, near Pagosa Springs. When they reached a place called Windy Pass, they took Fred Harman's ashes and scat-tered them across the land that the artist and so many others have called home.

That land was the Continental Divide.

Pavement

Most people who cover the state of New Mexico from top to bottom, or from bottom to top, take Interstate 25. It's a pleasant highway, fast and wide and clean-cut, but it's rather utilitarian. When I thought about traveling New Mexico, south to north, I wanted a course that would reveal the state, not just go through it. The solution came to me in a dream: N.M. 18.

N.M. 18 actually originates in Fort Stockton, Texas, and runs along New Mexico's east side almost to Colorado. I decided to pick it up at the extreme southeast corner of New Mexico. Dream became reality as I climbed in my car and started rolling. For two days in October, I followed a broken yellow stripe on a piece of pavement that most of the time was as straight as a table leg. My journey took me 439 miles, from the heat of lower New Mexico, where the elevation is 2,800 feet, to the cool, high plains north of Clayton, where N.M. 18 dead-ends at an altitude of 5,100 feet.

Traveling through five counties and two time zones, I went from oil to peanuts to cattle, from sandy lands to grasslands, and from dry stretches to drier: the average rainfall along N.M. 18 is fourteen to seventeen inches per year. Most of all I saw New Mexico's east flank, from toe to head. What I found was a body of land like no other. Except for some rolling stretches at the top of the state, 18 is flat. Its color varies: in some places it is slate black; in others salt and pepper; sometimes gray; even white. In one busy spot between Portales and Clovis, a mossy island runs down the middle of the pavement. But mostly 18 is a two-lane affair, divided by a golden dash.

Just south of Jal the still air is broken by the light thumping of pump jacks, those perpetual-motion machines some folks call oil wells. But the pump jacks have a different task; once the oil has been found, the pump jack does the rest, thumping along, pumping the oil into containers.

Somebody once described Jal as "tough as an old boot." However, the town also has a slick side, and nowhere is that more evident than at the Woolworth Community Library, a book's throw from N.M. 18. Everyone in Jal urges me to see "our library," which is about the fanciest structure in the Permian Basin. The library was built in 1977 at a cost of $1.1 million, a staggering sum when one considers that Jal's total population is but a few thousand souls.

The sandstone and red-brick structure was the gift of the late Elizabeth and May Woolworth, sisters who, curiously, never lived in Jal. Their brother and sister did, though, and the library was founded in their memory. Librarian Bobbi Martin leads me to a room containing Woolworth memorabilia. One item is the family Bible. "In their last years, the Woolworth women fretted their deaths wouldn't be recorded in this book," Martin explains. "They asked us not to start the library till they became the Bible's final entries. And of course we abided by their wishes."

North of Jal the landscape is painted with creosote bushes. Overhead an occasional hawk appears. Below, the highway is brown and undeviating. In Eunice, one of the main thoroughfares is named Texas Avenue. After all, in several places along 18, Texas is only a whisker away. Speaking of whiskers, shaves and haircuts in Eunice are done at the Cardinal Barber Shop. Like nearly every east-side community, little Eunice holds in great esteem its high school's mascot, in this case the cardinal. Thus there is the Cardinal Barber Shop. And Cardinal Drug. And the Redbird Gas Company.

Oil was first discovered in Lea County in 1922. There are now more than 12,000 oil and gas wells in the county, a figure that in 1982 helped New Mexico rank seventh among all states in crude oil production. The semi-arid, featureless Lea County oil fields have always been considered strictly a male bastion; the isolation, the stench, and the grime, and especially the bone-wearying labor, have never much appealed to women. However, a number of women have tried roustabouting, which entails lifting and lugging heavy pipes, and making repairs at oil leases. Most female roustabouts have quit. Near Eunice, standing alongside a jungle gym array of tubes and tanks, I find one who has been at it almost two years. "I've always liked outdoor work," says Nellie Armitige, wiping her glistening forehead with a blue bandanna. "And I need the job. I got five kids at home in Hobbs, and my husband's disabled." A large, black woman of thirty-three, Armitige works for the Atlantic Richfield Company. She says when she began the men on the gang were not ready for females. "One guy gave me a rough time, put me down and everything. But there is always somebody who makes you feel welcome, helps explain things." Armitige feels her moment of acceptance came the day she pulled her 200 pounds up a twenty-seven-foot ladder to the top of a heater-treater tower. "I proved something then." The acrid scent of oil and gas bothered Armitige at first, but now she says she is used to the smell. "My family still doesn't like it. When I take off my boots at home, they say, 'Ooh, you stink.' "

As I pull away, with Nellie Armitige in my rearview mirror holding a monkey wrench the length of a baseball bat, I notice that traffic in many places on 18 is light. The New Mexico Highway Department, in fact, says that at one spot on the highway, above Clayton, an average of only sixty cars per day passes by. Yet the people who ride this east-side road are generous. How can I tell? By the waves. Rural motorists everywhere like to signal howdy to oncoming cars. Usually this is done with two or three fingers. Along 18 I often get a whole hand.

Traveling through Hobbs, I turn my car radio to KHOB. The music heard most frequently on 18 is country. At high noon, on almost every station, the voice of newscaster Paul Harvey fills the airwaves. But on this station I hear the voice of a disk jockey with a most uncountry name: Seamus O'Connolly. Like many people in southeastern New Mexico, O'Connolly came from somewhere else—in his case, Connecticut—to work in the oil fields.

At the north end of Hobbs, where gas vats pop out of the ground like giant hatboxes, I stop by New Mexico Junior College to visit with Ron Black. Coach of the school's basketball team and a history professor, Black every summer leads a field trip called History 113A. The course is a whirlwind tour of New Mexico that takes students to twenty towns and more than seventy-five attractions in two weeks: if this is Tuesday, it must be Tucumcari.

Black tells me that his history-on-the-road itinerary includes visits to such out-of-the-way places as the Philmont Boy Scout Ranch near Cimarron, Montezuma Castle in Las Vegas, and the near-ghost town of Hillsboro, plus more popular ones such as the Sandia Peak Tram, the White Sands, and Kit Carson's home. "We try to stay off the beaten path," says Black, a neatly dressed, compact man. "We spend some time on little dirt roads, in tiny mountain towns, we stop by Penitente *moradas*. I've had some people from Santa Fe and Española on the tour and they tell me we've gone to places in northern New Mexico they hadn't seen before."

Normally, 60 percent of the people on the tour are schoolteachers. The course, which was started in 1971, is worth three hours of college credit. One student, Black recalls fondly, was an eighty-three-year-old woman, a retiree, and the oldest person to ever take the trip. "One evening, after we'd been hiking in Bandelier National Monument all day, I asked if anybody wanted to go into Santa Fe that night. Nobody did except this little old lady. She had incredible energy. Just ran the legs off everybody. When she rode up the chairlift at Red River, the operator, trying to be kind, turned off the lift to let her off. She was so furious she chewed that fellow out for a good five minutes."

The Shamrock Cafe ("just good food"), draws the attention of my eye and stomach in Lovington. Inside, I introduce myself to a young man with shoulder-length brown hair and a ready smile. Lonnie Berry tells me he has been in the oil fields—*awl feels*, he calls them—most of his life. He started out like Nellie Armitige, as a roustabout. "Then I was what they call 'lead tongs.' Then a chain hand, motorman, derrick man. Now I'm a driller. I could be a toolpusher next, but I can make more money drilling." Berry's work takes him up and down 18. For a year he drilled up the highway at Dora. He lives just off the highway in Lovington in a comfortable home with his wife, Janet, and daughter, Shayla Ra, three. "It's a good life," Berry says. "You're respected. Let's face it, oil's a necessity. You try to run that car of yours without it."

From Lovington, 18 begins a long straightaway, through Tatum, then past a number of crossroads, one named Crossroads. There is little else in Crossroads save the Wolf Wagon Works, a one-man business that rebuilds, restores, and repairs ancient buggies and other horse-drawn vehicles. Currently, John Wolf, the owner, is trying to sell a one-horse shay, circa 1870. It has two wheels, a black folding top, and green wool upholstery. Wolf is asking $4,500, plus tax.

As I try to envision clopping up 18 in a 100-year-old carriage, the highway shoots right through Highway, New Mexico. Surrounding me is the Llano Estacado, a shelf of sandhills. Needing gas, I turn off at the settlement of Milnesand, at the mercantile shop that has been run for forty-four years by Paul and Ethel Davis. Milnesand, Paul Davis tells me, acquired its name from a windmill that years before fell over and got stuck in one of 18's sandhills. The Davises' cozy shop specializes in guns. Shotgun shells, used scopes, and *Shooter's Bible*s overrun the counters. "We got quail, antelope, and dove around here," Davis explains. Living in Milnesand is healthy, according to his wife. "It keeps you young," she vouches. And sandy-haired.

When I reach Portales ("Home of 12,000 friendly folks and three or four grouches," boasts a billboard), I find the community getting ready for its annual Peanut Festival. Noting this, I pull off at Borden's, on the north edge of town. R. L. Borden meets me at the door of his plant. R. L.'s slow drawl, his sixty-eight years, and the ever-present toothpick in his mouth, are deceiving: his company is one of the biggest peanut processors in America. Borden's buys from the 400 peanut farmers in the area. Purchasing the crop in shells, Borden's cleans, packages, then sells the nuts, raw or roasted.

It takes only a moment for R. L. to get warmed up about the Valencia peanut, indigenous to the east side of New Mexico. "It's the best-flavored peanut grown anywhere," he says. "You can get a test to prove me right." I ask R. L. about the Peanut Festival. It's an arts and crafts fair, and a talent show and has games such as foot racing with a peanut in a spoon, he says. The festival is held every October, during harvest season. Peanuts are planted in May. I wonder how R. L. manages to run with a spoon and a toothpick in his mouth. When I ask him, he tells me he has never been to the festival. "Always too busy." Another surprise: health problems have stopped R. L. from eating peanuts. This does not keep him from showing me how to open one. With thumb and forefinger of one hand, he presses firmly along the seam of a three-pod Valencia shell until it splits apart evenly. He hands me the nuts. "Good," I offer after a moment. R. L. smiles.

Halfway between Portales and Clovis stands the Blackwater Draw Museum, dedicated to early man. At age sixty-three, George Agogino, the museum's director, may be the rarest specimen in the place. Agogino is mastodonic in profile. His white hair runs wild, and his leisure suits are pale blue. A part-time hypnotist who drives an ancient, battered red Karmann Ghia, Agogino designed the museum in the shape of an arrowhead. Some of the museum's exhibits come from Agogino's personal collection—from trips he has made throughout the world. Two objects he procured from an unusual archaeological site: Hollywood. The pieces are twelve-foot-long spears Agogino spotted on the old "Star Trek" television show. While they may not be prehistoric, the spears, Agogino felt, were good likenesses of the ones used by people who roamed the earth 100 centuries ago. So Agogino wrote to Universal Studios and the spears were his. Agogino says he took a lot of flak for the spears, but the schoolkids who visit the museum love them.

Big bronze busts made to resemble Paleo-Indian people sit on pedestals. "Somebody made them," says Agogino, stopping at one bust. He laughs. "Somebody made this guy look a little like Christ." Cardboard models covered with glue stand in one corner. A group of mammoth molars rests under glass. "The teeth are casts," explains Agogino. "You make 'em the same way you do false teeth."

Drivers cruising 18 can recognize an approaching community by the town's water tower. The silver tank is usually the tallest structure around. In Clovis, the highway's halfway point, the tallest thing in town belongs to the Curry County Grain and Elevator Company.

Clovis may be the biggest city on 18, but in other ways it is like all communities along the highway: its sports teams are prized, and with good reason. They're invariably first-rate, including Marshall Junior High School, "Home of the Flying Kittens." Clovis is proud, too, of its churches, as are all east-side towns. On Fridays, the daily newspaper's religion section runs three full pages. There are more than sixty churches of all denominations.

As the monstrous grain elevator suggests, agriculture is important to Clovis. Restaurants second this notion. There are a dozen steakhouses in town. "Corn-fed steaks," brags one. In the mid-1960s, Clovis was the site of the first K-Bob's Steak House anywhere. Allsup's, the bread and milk convenience store chain also started here. Clearly then, there is no excuse for leaving Clovis hungry—spiritually or physically.

There is also no excuse to leave Clovis without acquiring a knowledge of rock 'n' roll. During the late 1950s, just off Clovis's Main Street, which 18 becomes, singer Buddy Holly recorded most of his greatest hits, including "That'll Be the Day" and "Peggy Sue." Holly lived in Lubbock, Texas, at the time, but Clovis had one of the best musical arrangers and sound technicians in the country in Norman Petty. Petty is gone now, and his studio is a shell of its former self. But Bob Linville, a vocalist who used to sing backup for Holly and tour with his band, the Crickets, is very much alive. He works as the assistant manager of Clovis's TG&Y, a store that happens to look out upon a busy N.M. 18.

In 1958, Petty backgrounded Holly's music with a group called the Roses, three college kids from Odessa, Texas. The Roses can be heard on several Holly singles, including the popular "It's So Easy." Now forty-eight, portly, and balding, Linville recorded and toured with Holly for about a year. He received no royalties. "What I got out of it," he says, "was the most fun in my life." On tour with Holly in Norfolk, Virginia, Linville received from the singer a gift of two guitar picks. He still has them—in a Clovis bank's safe-deposit box.

The Roses were living in a Clovis apartment on February 3, 1959, the day Holly died in a plane crash in Iowa. Linville says he got up that morning, turned on the television, and saw Holly's face. "I'll never get over that as long as I live. I felt that a good friend was gone." After Holly's death, Linville went into the Army. Upon returning to Clovis he worked for Norman Petty for a year or so and then went into the merchandising business. Like many big stores, the Clovis TG&Y does well with Buddy Holly tapes and records. And though the store's assistant manager is on some of those tapes and records, few people know it. "I know, though," Linville says. "And that's good enough for me."

N.M. 18 is a road not only of scenes but of scents. North of Clovis the smell of fertilizer is strong. Here the highway has grown a most peculiar feature: two ninety-degree turns to Tucumcari. Comanches ranged this prairie once. Now there is milo and abandoned homesteads. Many east-side communities were founded in the early 1900s. Some, like Clovis, which will soon be eighty years old, have expanded enormously. Others, like tiny Broadview, hang on. Even without a stoplight, Grady survives. Its water tower tells me so: "Home of the Broncos, 1980 State Champions."

On this section of 18 there are often more windmills than people. All the windmills, I notice, are made by Aermotor, and most of the devices have fifteen blades. So much for roadside trivia. Just north of Quay, a historic marker tells me that this was the spot where Black Jack Ketchum, the bandit who terrorized railroads in the late 1800s, killed two men, then hid in a nearby cave. Though the highway's current route was established in 1932, long after Ketchum's death, I sense that I might meet his ghost.

Tucumcari has button-busting pride. Hobbs may be the "Home of the People Pleasers," and Lovington "the Little City with a Big Heart," but Tucumcari is the "Cowchip Capital of New Mexico." Civic pride is evident in how 18 crosses Tucumcari: the highway bisects a shopping center. Completed in the mid-1970s for half a million dollars, Tucumcari's Downtown Mall is urban renewal at its best. Instead of neglecting the inner city, Tucumcari overhauled three blocks on Main Street and wound up with dozens of tidy shops set among rock gardens and atriums. It may flaunt cowchips, but Tucumcari has charm.

Just south of Logan, my trail traverses the Canadian, the biggest river on the east side. The Canadian is grand, but I find something in Logan nearly as eye-catching: a mural painted on the outside of the Casa Blanca Motel. The oddly placed artwork was done twenty-five years ago by Manuel Acosta, a former pupil of Peter Hurd. Scenes on the thirty-foot-long motel siding depict various events in New Mexico history. I make a mental note to tell Ron Black of the sprawling tableau. He might wish to add Logan to his tour. The mural was designed by Joe Hettinger, once proprietor of the Casa Blanca. *Time Marches On* is the title.

My time is marching on, too. A clock in a gas station at Nara Visa indicates that it is an hour later than what my wristwatch says. I have always thought that every location in New Mexico was on the same time. I ask the station's owner, a stout gent named Curley, about this. Curley explains that Nara Visa is the only spot in the state on Central Standard Time, or "Texas Time," as he calls it. "It's been that way long as I can remember," Curley muses. "It started when they put in the Rock Island Railroad through here. When they took out the depot, the time stayed like it was. I s'pose people are used to it. I never heard otherwise."

Another as-far-as-the-eye-can-see piece of 18 extends from Nara Visa to Clayton. This stretch cleaves the Kiowa National Grasslands, a region so shimmering that I feel as if I am driving on a sea of sheets. Farther along, I spot a lonely pickup, and next to that, a single figure hunkered near the roadside. The man's straw hat is pushed back to reveal a young, sunburnt face. His hands sift what is left of the summer soil. He is scowling. Joe Clavel raises cattle near Yates. This was not a good summer for him. Range caterpillars went through his acreage like pigs in a corn trough. Clavel, thirty-one, says he used to spray with toxaphene, until the Environmental Protection Agency outlawed it. Since then he has been spraying with the much less effective dylox. "Didn't do a damn bit of good," Clavel says, tossing down the shredded grass.

Federal grasslands checkerboard private and state lands in this corner of New Mexico. In 1972, when range caterpillars showed up in full force for the first time, the federal government refused to spray its own land. The untreated plots infested the surrounding area, including Joe Clavel's ranch. In the past decade, range caterpillars have caused more than $40 million in losses to New Mexico cattle growers. Simply, the pest can survey a section of prime grazing grass and in no time become a member of the clean plate club. "Economically, it's an impossibility for me to foot all the bills and spray my land, too," says Clavel. "I'm expecting a better beef market next year and that's the only reason I'm willing to spray." Clavel has been ranching only five years. "It feels like a lifetime."

Twenty-five miles south of Clayton, I ease off the highway at the hamlet of Stead. Stead used to feature a garage and general store. Today there is only a post office. It is looked after by an amiable, platinum-haired woman named Gracie Cornell, who seems genuinely glad to see a stranger. She says that Stead has twenty-four residents, most of whom raise cattle and maize. The post office is open for just two hours a day, every day except Sunday. What sort of mail do Steadites receive? "Oh, they get turkeys and fruit at Christmas," says Cornell. "And all the other times, bills."

On its way to Clayton's Main Street, traffic on 18 rolls past the formidable, silver-domed Union County Courthouse. Arriving in town, I decide to eat at the Eklund Hotel. The Eklund, I discover, was constructed in 1892. Although its beds aren't open for business, its restored saloon is. Here I enjoy an excellent hamburger and meet up again with Black Jack Ketchum, as I knew I might. The Eklund's tavern is Black Jack's Beanery. It is warm and dark and equipped with a well-tuned color television. Patrons receive napkins decorated with cattle brands from across the state. But Ketchum is the bar's star. Clippings and photographs of his exploits dot the walls. Several pictures record poor Black Jack's death—he was hung in Clayton in 1901.

A postprandial stroll through Clayton takes me past the Luna Theater. Its exterior—a large, funky moon face on the roof—grabs my interest. Rosalie Garcia, a short, dark-haired woman, is sitting in the theater's cashier booth doing paperwork. I ask her about the face on the roof. *Luna* means "moon" in Spanish, she says with a smile. Of course, I nod. Garcia began sacking popcorn at the Luna when she was fourteen. Twenty-seven years and four children later she's the manager. All that time she has worked at the theater six nights a week. Wednesdays, she's off. Drudgery? Not on your life, she says. "Every Wednesday from 7:00 to 9:00 P.M. I get really bored." This dedication adds up to around 2,500 motion pictures, give or take some double features. "People say to me, 'I bet you've seen a lot of movies.' I haven't. When my work is done—selling tickets, counting money—I come in and sit down in the back. I've seen the ending of lots of movies."

The Luna's face fascinates me, but so does the fact that the theater is part of a growing trend: a last picture show. The National Association of Theater Owners says that there are 106 indoor movie houses in New Mexico. There used to be many more; every small town used to have one. The Luna survives, but not easily. "What really has hurt us is that HBO," sighs Garcia. "In the winter, everybody stays home. In the summer, everybody rushes around. It's a shame. This is such a pretty theater. Look at our beautiful gold molding inside." According to Garcia, people in Clayton aren't informed enough about movies. "We'd get more customers if there were write-ups in the local paper about the movies we show. We'd get even more people if the movies had better language."

Clovis may be the "Cattle Capital of the Southwest," but Clayton is the "Cattle Center of the West." Up the highway from the sprawling, malodorous cattle pens is perhaps the most remote roadway in New Mexico. Only an occasional "stock on highway" sign breaks the terrain. This is twister territory; the state's meanest tornadoes have touched down in this isolated corner. Few human forms are seen on this part of the highway. But make no mistake: the land is inhabited. Onto various fields along the road someone has wheeled giant rotary sprinklers that look like oversized clothes racks.

Nineteen miles northeast of Clayton is the last stop on 18. It's a place called Moses, not a stop really, unless you happen to live here, and only six persons do. Moses is actually two places: Old Moses and, for several years, a suburb known as New Moses. Without fanfare, 18 terminates only eight miles from Colorado. An intersection offers motorists a choice. The road east goes to Oklahoma, two miles away—the one west to Folsom, New Mexico. If this is an end, it is also a beginning. By turning around, I can go back down the pavement. Back down the east side. Back down the road of sights and smells and dreams.

III

Junctions

Lucky

Should the average working stiff require a pack of Rolaids, chances are he goes to his corner drugstore in a '77 Datsun with a dent in the door. When Lucky Boyd's tummy hurts, he climbs in the back of a twenty-six-foot-long, midnight-blue limousine, then orders his chauffeur to fetch the antacids. Lucky Boyd spells relief *F-L-A-U-N-T*.

It is morning and I am sitting in the crushed-velvet rear seat of a luxury limo, a stretch as it is called in the trade. We are parked in front of Walgreens, in Albuquerque's Coronado Center. Lucky Boyd's full-time chauffeur, a gaunt version of Arthur Treacher, has gone into the drugstore on a Rolaids mission. Facing me is Lucky's assistant, a young woman named Joan Mott. When strangers see Joan idling in the big car, they often think she's a movie actress. Joan isn't; she's from New Jersey, but don't hold that against her.

Alongside me in the limo is the real star, a huge man in a Day-Glo dark suit: Lucky. At the moment, Lucky is on the telephone, a $4,000 phone. He is talking to someone in Dallas, Texas. At our feet is a well-stocked bar and a fifteen-inch color television set. "As the World Turns" is coming on.

"How y'all doin'?" Lucky booms into the telephone. Where the average working stiff talks in moderate tones, Lucky booms. Into each of his words he puts every one of his 280 pounds. Outside, in the

Walgreens parking lot, people stare. The gawkers can't glimpse much; the limo's windows are darkened. People peer in anyhow. Such a monstrous car with a uniformed manservant is a rare sight in Albuquerque. Who could be inside? It can't be Willie or Waylon; the State Fair hasn't opened. It can't be the Pope; the car doesn't look bulletproof. And besides, what limousine owner shops at Walgreens? Lucky Boyd, that's who.

"I gotta be different," Lucky whispers in a voice that resounds like a Sansui speaker. Lucky goes to public places, he confesses, to impress people, to watch their reactions. Traveling incognito is not his style. "This here car is my way of being different. This here car is my way of saying, 'I'm Lucky Boyd.' "

In an effort to discover just who Lucky Boyd is, rubberneckers have been known to drive their own cars off the road. The curious have been known to follow Lucky's limo for miles, just to find out who is inside. When those same snoopy souls finally corner Lucky's sepulchral-looking driver, George Fahlbusch, the conversation frequently goes something like this:

"Who do you work for?"

"Mr. Boyd."

"Boyd? . . . What's he do?"

"*Mistah* Boyd runs the Rio Rancho Inn."

There may not exist a better conversation stopper than that: "he runs the Rio Rancho Inn." The Rio Rancho Inn! And it's all perfectly true. But still, a guy who runs the Rio Rancho Inn needs a chauffeured limo with a rosewood bar and a Pulsar phone and a Sony tube and two fridges, like a guy who runs Ace Dry Cleaners needs a customized dirigible.

Yet the limo, a Cadillac Fleetwood, is one of the few, perhaps the only, privately owned, round-the-clock-tended coaches in town. Popping a Rolaids, Lucky says, with great understatement, "This here car gets me where I want to go."

On this here particular day, now that his stomach has begun to feel better, Lucky announces where he wants to go: to lunch. Joan Mott, Lucky's Gal Friday by way of Jersey, suggests a French place. Lucky has other ideas. "George," he calls for nearly half the world to hear, "George, take us to Top Dog."

Ronald Reagan may never make it to Top Dog. But according to Lucky, Reagan is a good friend. Lucky says Reagan used the limo as a decoy during a visit to Albuquerque. Lucky says that he bought the car last year from Jim Garner, the actor. Lucky says he paid $60,000 for it, and that it's a 1982 model. Since Lucky has owned the car, heads of state have placed their bottoms on the limo's back seats, which cost $15,000 alone. Prince Charles has roosted in the stretch. So has Teddy Yip. Teddy Yip? You don't know Teddy Yip? Lucky is amazed. Heck, Teddy's that billionaire with fifty-two wives. Lucky loaned Teddy $400. One of Teddy's girlfriends needed pocket money.

Bill Holden, the actor, never hitched a ride in Lucky's car. But Holden did, Lucky claims, once throw a birthday party for Lucky in Nogales. "I know everybody," Lucky boasts.

When we arrive at Top Dog, a fast-food eatery on Menaul Boulevard that specializes in frankfurters and has tables the size of throat lozenges, it is evident the restaurant's parking lot was not designed for twenty-six-foot automobiles. Never mind; George is an expert at maneuvering big boats. After all, Lucky says, George has steered the car to Las Vegas a couple of times. After all, last April George drove Lucky to Washington, D.C. Lucky needed to see some guy named Reagan. After all, Lucky knows everybody.

Between bites of a Polish sausage lathered in extra-hot mustard, Lucky talks about the person he knows best. He was born, he says, in 1931 in a state that seems appropriate: Texas. His birth certificate indicates he is Luther Merrel Boyd. Nobody calls him that. *Nobody*. Years back, while shooting craps in Vegas, Lucky got on a roll. "You're lucky," a casino patron observed. The name stuck. It now adorns his limo's license plate, his $900 belt buckle, and anything else that can be held down for branding.

Are you still lucky? someone asks. "Tell you what," Lucky answers, digging into some French fries, "I'm more smart than lucky. Smart because I do my thinking while other people are sleeping."

It wasn't his parents who taught Lucky that trick—to think while others slept; Lucky was orphaned early. And it wasn't a teacher, either; Lucky never got beyond the seventh grade. A native of Fort Worth, Texas, Lucky claims he learned survival and get-ahead methods as a twelve-year-old Marine in World War II. (He says he snuck into the service by "borrowing" a notary's seal.) Later, in the early 1950s, he took a job as a kitchen steward for $11.59 a week at the Los Angeles, California, Hilton. He stayed with the Hilton chain, went to every school it offered, applied himself, worked hard, and did a whole lot of thinking while others napped. In time he became a manager. Lucky arrived in Albuquerque in 1966 to run the old Hilton. He got to know everybody in town—the Unser brothers, politicos, big shots, little blasts. He made some good investments and refined the art of flaunting. A couple of years ago Lucky bought into the Rio Rancho Inn. He has turned it into a successful hotel. Why Rio Rancho? "Hey!" booms Lucky. "Rio Rancho—that's God's country."

It is time to leave Top Dog. In the limousine, "The Price Is Right" is winding down, and the contents of an ice bucket have melted. But here is the real crisis: a fly has found its way into the car, and George has forgotten to pack a swatter.

The fly doesn't slow Lucky from getting back on the telephone. He dials Steve Anaya, the governor's nephew and manager of the New Mexico State Fair. Lucky loves money; he admits it. He loves politics almost as much. Especially Republican politics. Never mind that Anaya is a Democrat. "I love to call up politicians," Lucky says. "I help them and they help me. I don't want to be in the limelight; I just want an ear. I know everybody. I knew Pete Domenici when Pete was an attorney in Albuquerque with eight kids and a '57 Chevy station wagon that he had to jump-start to get to work every day."

Lucky's limo would never need a boost. Lucky babies the car. Only George is allowed to drive it; Lucky rarely climbs behind the wheel. Should the limo receive a scratch, George has the car repainted. The paint costs $100 a quart. Lucky calls his car "the Big Eye Doctor." It sees and knows everything. A window on the world. Lucky's world.

While Lucky talks to Anaya about the State Fair's Beach Boys concert ("I know them boys, sure"), George Fahlbusch takes a cigarette break. George is a retired cop from Long Island, New York. He has been driving for Lucky for a year. George loves his job. The highlight was, of course, the trip to the White House to see Lucky's good friend. George says the President's limousine isn't as good as Mr. Boyd's. Mr. Boyd's limo, George says, has everything the President's has, except one thing: a red button. George says Mr. Boyd may try to get one of them red buttons next week.

"Guiding Light" is going strong when Lucky finishes with Anaya. The afternoon sun catches a big rock on Lucky's left hand. "Four carats," Lucky reports. "I do love diamonds." Lucky may enjoy the good things in life, like J&B Scotch and turtle-skin boots and flashy gems. Lucky may be somewhat of a show-off and more than a bit of a ham. But Lucky has a flip side. It's a tune that he doesn't play loudly.

Lucky's limo is not for rent, nor is George for hire. Yet Lucky will loan the car and his chauffeur—at no cost—to folks in need. When a friend needs a ride to the doctor, Lucky sends over the Big Eye Doctor. When an Indian leader from out of town requires some wheels in Albuquerque, Lucky hands over his. When an unemployed crony has a job interview lined up, Lucky dispatches George to pick up and deliver the fellow. An inveterate checkgrabber, perennial giftgiver, and pal to stray animals, Lucky Boyd has a heart the size of a spare tire. It wasn't always that way, however.

The turning point came in 1964, when Lucky's son, Charles, was wounded in Vietnam. Hospitalized in Kansas, Charles telephoned his father with some dreadful news: doctors wanted to amputate both of Charles's legs. "Don't let them do it, Dad!" he begged. At the time, Lucky was managing a Hilton in Denver, Colorado. He knew lots of people even then. One of his friends, a Republican politician, not surprisingly, was Peter Dominick, the U.S. senator from Colorado. Hearing of Lucky's dilemma, Dominick stepped in and had Charles flown to specialists at Fitzsimmons Army Hospital in Denver. Twenty-three operations later Charles Boyd walked out of Fitzsimmons—on his own legs. "That changed me," says Lucky. "Before that I was all for Lucky. I never helped people until then. I never knew how good it could make a person feel, until somebody helped me."

There is perhaps no one Lucky wants to help out more than Bobby Unser. Lucky and Billye Boyd, his wife of thirty-six years, live next door to the race car driver. Lucky is an unabashed Bobby Unser fan, an admirer with total devotion. When Unser throws a victory party, Lucky can be counted on to bring the champagne— and the laughs.

When Bobby Unser is out of town, and he is a great deal, Lucky watches the Unser place. On this day Bobby is in Alaska, so Lucky needs to check on things. Lucky also needs to stop by his own house. He needs to get that fly swatter.

Bobby Unser's house looks okay to Lucky. The three bearskin rugs, thick enough to break an ankle on, still cover the floor. A shotgun case next to Bobby and Marsha Unser's bed is intact. An STP-decal bedspread is in its place. "Bobby's a great guy," Lucky says, tapping the bedspread. "Want me to call him on the telephone from the car? I can make a conference call. We got speakers in the car."

We decide not to call Alaska. Instead, we set out for Academy Furniture Mart. The store's owner, Ron Turner, wants Lucky to park the limo out front for a while to attract customers. Turner is a friend and for friends Lucky will do most anything. To get to Academy Furniture, George drives through Corrales. "Eight is Enough" has begun. "Look at them houses," Lucky says, pointing to Corrales estates worth seven figures. "They look so junky to me. How can people live in them?"

Ron Turner was right: the limo's engine is still warm when a crowd begins to gather outside Academy Furniture. A pleased Turner scrunches his long frame into the car. The furniture store owner picks up the car's telephone. "Hey, Lucky," he says with a conspiratorial grin. "How do I get an overseas operator?" Lucky starts to show him.

As the limo pulls away finally, Lucky telephones the Rio Rancho Inn. The Rio Rancho Inn! Business is good, he's told. Satisfied, Lucky opens a miniature bottle of chilled Inglenook wine. With his other hand he shoves an Eddy Arnold tape into a tape player. The television he doesn't touch; it's tuned to "Happy Days."

The din within the limo, combined with the Inglenook, causes Lucky's guest to nod off. No sleep for Lucky, though. Not while others are snoozing. That's Lucky's time to think.

Mandibles

Did you hear the one about the Hobbs alligator who was late getting home from work? He'd been swamped.

Alligator jokes aren't heard much these days in Hobbs. Seems the alligators down here have pulled a see-you-later. Even the crocodiles have been gone for a while. Oh, there's still one 'gator out at the sewage plant. But that's a small number for a town once known as the Everglades of the Permian Basin.

Though there were never as many alligators in Hobbs as, say, there are seals in Nome, Alaska, there once were enough in the land-locked, carcass-dry city to cause quite a stir. Enough to cause one city official to suggest maybe Hobbs ought to start a shoe factory. And yet trying to find an alligator in Hobbs today is about as easy as trying to brush the creature's teeth. The Animal House, over in the Broadmoor Mall, peddles parrots and boa constrictors, but no baby 'gators. Papillon, a Hobbs boutique that bills itself as "the most comprehensive ladies store in New Mexico," hasn't stocked an alligator handbag in eons. Why, Papillon doesn't even carry those preppy designer duds adorned with tiny reptiles. It would be dandy to report an Albert E. Gaiter listed in the Hobbs telephone directory. But there isn't.

Right about now you're probably thinking this whole story is a big croc. If so, you need only check the records, which begin with an evening in March 1972. It was then that two Hobbs city employees made a name for themselves at the old sewage plant.

First a word or two about Hobbs sewage. The stuff has had an up-and-down history. In 1966, Hobbs received a plaque from a Las Cruces group. "Best sewer system in New Mexico," the commendation read. Seven years later Hobbs was sued by the state's Environmental Improvement Agency. Allegedly, the community's stellar sewage system was causing the pollution of ninety-two private wells. Prior to the mid-1970s, Hobbs sewage was treated in lagoons in the southeast part of town. There were nearly a dozen lagoons, each about three feet deep and interconnected. Daily, more than 2 million gallons of effluent was dumped into the lagoons from the sewage plant.

If all this sounds rather malodorous, it wasn't. The old plant was a fairly pleasant place to work. Two workers, John Vanderventer and Roger Tison, found something unusual there back in March 1972. As they were preparing to leave for the day, the pair spotted in a drainage ditch what looked like an especially long lizard. They pursued it on foot, and when they caught it, they knew it was no lizard. "We got an alligator out here," one of the men telephoned the sewage center's supervisor, Jake Morgan. Morgan is a Hobbs native; he knew alligators were not. In fact, Morgan knew they didn't belong anywhere near the Staked Plains of southeastern New Mexico. "You boys been drinkin'?" Morgan asked.

The alligator, a toddler measuring thirty-three inches, was no hallucination. And when news of its presence spread, the switchboard at Hobbs City Hall lighted up like the aurora borealis. "Kill that 'gator," threatened one caller, "and y'all will burn in hell." The decision to keep the alligator was not a difficult one. Though alligators have been waddling about for 70 million years, the critters were facing extinction in the wild when the two workers spotted one in Hobbs. Only a few years before, the U.S. Department of the Interior had placed alligators on the endangered species list. While that act caused the alligator population to swell suddenly in states like Florida and Texas, in New Mexico alligators were and always have been about as plentiful as gila monsters at the North Pole. Therefore, they shouldn't be touched. Period.

So the Hobbs alligator was spared. And it was given a name. John Roger Enzymes, he became, though it never would be clear if indeed he was a he or a she. The "John Roger" part of the name was for the two city employees. "Enzymes" was for the organic substance produced by the sewage plant. Later, when "Enzymes" was dropped, no one really complained.

Discovered at the sewage plant, John Roger would be kept there. All sorts of people in Hobbs immediately offered their services to make his life at the plant more palatable. The Rose Gravel Company donated bags of concrete, and a little swimming hole was dug. Farmers kicked in chicken wire, and a cage was built. Instantly, John Roger became one of Hobbs's top attractions. Schoolchildren flocked to see him. Someone suggested the community adopt him as a mascot. Morale at the sewage plant soared.

Then in June 1972, three months after he was found, John Roger turned up missing. "Gatornapped!" cried the *Hobbs Daily News-Sun*. Four days later, after a frantic search, John Roger was found in a lagoon 200 feet from his home. A double layer of chicken wire was ordered placed around and atop his cage. A sewage worker was assigned to check the cage periodically. In time, John Roger came to accept his new home, even if it wasn't by the bayou.

If you think this concludes the story of reptiles in Hobbs, you're wrong by a large scale. In September 1972, a Hobbs schoolteacher awoke one morning to find in his back yard a two-pound crocodile. How did anyone know it was a crocodile? As one policeman with a downhome sense of dentistry put it, "Alligators got an overbite; crocodiles got an underlap."

The crocodile was put in the same cage as John Roger. The two didn't get along because the croc didn't much like anyone. In fact, he wanted to press his underlapping lips on all who came near. A few weeks later, he died, nameless. If any tears were shed, it's not known if they were the crocodile kind.

Less than a year had passed when two more Hobbs city employees found still another creature, this one an alligator, on the Eunice Highway south of town. This 'gator was 2½ feet long and appeared to have political clout. Instead of being named for two maintenance workers, he was called Billy Max, in honor of two conservation-minded city commissioners, William Rash and Max Clampitt. Billy Max spent that first night in a shower stall at the Hobbs Police Station. "Someone might claim him," a cop explained. When no one did, Billy Max was taken to—where else?—the sewage plant. He would room with John Roger.

The two alligators lived together happily until 1977 when the chicken wire gave way, and Billy Max bolted. His bones were found alongside one of the lagoons. "Check so-and-so's garage," an anonymous caller whispered to Hobbs utilities director Arky Wheeler. "You'll find that 'gator's skin on the wall." Wheeler, who never cared to play hide-and-seek, declined to follow up the tip.

Not long after Billy Max died, there occurred in Hobbs the Great Alligator Scare. This was immediately followed by the Great Alligator Hunt. One more city employee, this one named Richard Lewis, stepped down off his tractor one day near a sewage lagoon and came face to face with what Lewis later breathlessly claimed was "an eight-foot 'gator sunning himself." Not wishing to break out his Coppertone, Lewis fled fast.

The Great Scare kicked off the Great Hunt. If there really were more creatures in the brackish lagoons, as Richard Lewis swore there were, authorities said they should be found. Hobbs's sewage treatment plant would soon convert to enclosed evaporative tanks. The lagoons would be bulldozed. No one wanted to bury an alligator. There was another reason for beginning the Great Hunt. An animal shelter was going to be built near the sewage treatment facility. 'Gators, someone pointed out, liked nothing better than to dine on beagle or tabby.

When word of the Great Alligator Hunt got out, the phone lines at Hobbs City Hall once again rang without mercy. Nearly forty persons offered to help. The first night of the Great Hunt turned into a carnival. A fleet of flat-bottom boats was launched onto the sewage lagoons. Men carrying nooses, sandwiches, radios, and guitars trolled the murky waters. By the following evening, the hunters had been reduced by half. The hootenanny had cooled. A voice of reason had stepped in. The voice belonged to Tom Salb, a Hobbs High School biology teacher. When he was a graduate student in Texas, Salb had actually done some alligator hunting. He quietly told Hobbs city officials that he appreciated all the assistance. But because of the commotion on the lagoons, Salb explained, an alligataor wasn't going to poke up its snout—even if "Crocodile Rock" came on the radio.

With a smaller crew, Salb continued the search. He found lots of snakes but not one alligator or crocodile, not even a rubber toy one. "They're in there," insisted Roy Riddle, the city's environmental supervisor. "The moon's keeping them away," argued someone else. "They've gone into the mud to hibernate," decided Salb. "They can live in the mud without food for three or four months." Two weeks after it began, the Great Hunt was called off. The lagoons were bulldozed. If there was an alligator in them, it received an expensive grave: the new sewage treatment facility cost $7.5 million.

It is at the rear of Hobbs's purple-brick Wastewater Reclamation Facility that John Roger, now eleven years old, resides. He has grown— fifty-seven inches at last measure. And he weighs nearly 100 pounds. Jake Morgan, the sewage plant supervisor who questioned the sobriety of John Roger's discoverers, has been keeper of the reptile since the beginning. "He'll eat just about anything you throw at him that's alive," says Morgan. Snakes, toads, salamanders, lizards, turtles, and grasshoppers dominate the menu. From his pocket, Morgan pulls the white-plate special: a bag of Kraft marshmallows. "Here, John Roger," Morgan coos. "Here, boy." Before you can say alley-oop, the sweets vanish, bag and all.

Long-nosed and leathery, Jake Morgan appears the perfect alligator handler. Indeed, Morgan, fifty-four, looks as if he once rassled 'gators. He wouldn't tangle with John Roger, though. John Roger once chewed a sewage worker's finger. However, that was a long time ago. Morgan says John Roger likes to do his own killing. "It's sort of terrible to watch," Morgan relates. "I mean, he's so shrewd. We've put chickens in his pen, and he sneaks up on them and pops 'em down in one bite." Equally dangerous is John Roger's tail. "It's pretty stout," says Morgan, tossing more marshmallows. "It'll whack you good upside the head."

When the new sewage treatment center was completed, John Roger received new digs. His house is a chocolate-colored half-barrel, a donation from the Unichem Corporation of Hobbs. His twelve-by-fifteen-foot playground features high grass and low concrete. A six-foot-high, chain-link fence keeps John Roger from ending up like Billy Max.

Most days John Roger spends in a pool that fronts his Unichem barrel. The water is rank with algae. "Dirtier the better," explains Morgan. Somehow, John Roger has never been sick a day. Periodically, he will disappear under the green slime for as long as twenty minutes. A great deal of the time, however, he lies just below the water's surface, his eyes forming a periscope. Morgan says when John Roger looks up, he is hungry. Morgan says when John Roger looks up and hisses simultaneously, be on guard; he is extra hungry. Morgan takes pains to note that John Roger doesn't freeload; Hobbs's taxpayers don't foot his food bills. His meals are provided by citizen gifts or by sewage department workers and other city employees who happen onto edibles in the field.

An average of six visitors a day stop by to see John Roger. Nearly once a week a school bus of tots pulls up for a look. Unfortunately,

John Roger does not easily warm up to strangers, even little ones. He has, it seems, only a one-word vocabulary: *gurk*. Frequently, John Roger refuses to speak at all or even be seen. This often annoys visitors, since there is little else to do at the sewage plant. Feeling cheated, onlookers occasionally try to get the alligator's attention. The sewage department discourages this. A sign above John Roger's cage warns, "Please don't throw rocks."

At the end of October each year, Morgan lassos John Roger with a couple of choker cables, swings the 'gator into a pickup, and chauffeurs him over to the sewage plant's primary pump station. There, John Roger is deposited in an old bathtub with about two inches of water and a screen cover. It's hibernation time; he'll sleep till April. One winter Morgan kept John Roger in his pen and used sun lamps to warm him. John Roger didn't like it. He prefers the bathtub. John Roger doesn't like to come out of hibernation, either. "When he wakes up," says Morgan, "it's always on the wrong side of the tub."

If an alligator in Hobbs is like an armadillo in Greenland, how did all the 'gators wind up where they did? Jake Morgan figures people purchased the reptiles as babies in Florida, then took them home to New Mexico. When the animals got too big, the owners, not wishing to destroy them, dumped the tiny pets in the old sewage lagoons.

There exists a possibility, though slim, that the Hobbs alligators and crocodiles were disposed of with a flush of a toilet. *Alligator*, a satirical movie of a few years ago, advanced this notion. The film tells of a 'gator which, put down a potty, grows to gigantic proportions in a city's sewer system. After escaping from its cesspool, the beast begins to swallow Chryslers. Most sewage experts, however, say an alligator wouldn't make it underground: there aren't enough marshmallows.

With the lagoons in Hobbs now gone, it would seem logical the creatures who inhabited them would be gone, too, right? Maybe. Seems there is a man-made lake north of Hobbs called Green Meadows. Seems that a couple of neighbors in the area complained that their dogs had suddenly disappeared. The neighbors even began to blame an animal they said lived in the depths of Green Meadows. "Charlie," they called the animal, and they said it was an overgrown catfish. Other Hobbs residents shook their heads knowingly at this news. There is, they protested, only one kind of catfish that can eat a dog. That's a dark green one, with an overbite—or an underlap.

More than seven feet long now, John Roger continues to thrive at the sewage plant. He was recently given a new hibernation den to replace his old bathtub. The swanky, sun-heated canopy is courtesy of Solar Age of Hobbs.

Deep Thinkers

During the spring of 1962, when people feared the Russians were going to level southeastern New Mexico, the town of Artesia turned a cotton patch into a combination underground school and bomb shelter. What has happened in two decades? Well, southeastern New Mexico has yet to be nuked, and the first subterranean school in the world is still down there, leaks and all.

"Go on up to Thirteenth Street, hang a left, and follow the signs." An Artesia gas station attendant is giving directions to Abo (pronounced *Ah-bow*) Elementary School in a manner that suggests he has done so many times before. "Can't miss it," he adds. But you can, especially if you're not looking for a gray, half-size football field, studded with three telephone-booth-like entrances leading below ground.

Twenty years after the last mound of soil was smoothed over, Abo School continues to attract visitors. Hard as it is to find, the place is still one of the best-known elementary schools in America. "Had some educators in from Indiana just yesterday," says Albert Bach. Bach, forty-seven, has been Abo's principal and head cheerleader since 1969. Ushering guests beneath twenty-one inches of concrete and several feet of dirt to the school, Bach rattles off in a homey twang the building's advantages: "no windows to wash, no noise, no dust. Why, we hardly have any vandalism at all." An Artesia native, Bach is a dark-haired, bespectacled man who seasons his sentences with words like "dadgummit" and "sucker." Behind his desk is a wooden plank inscribed "Board of Education." "Dadgummit," says Bach, "I tell the kids here that they're *not* going to get spanked with that sucker if they climb up on the roof." That is Albert Bach's favorite joke: anyone can climb on Abo's roof because the concrete top is the school's playground.

Roswell architect Frank Standhart dreamed up the whole thing. He got the idea in the late 1950s. Having already designed windowless schools in the area, Standhart had an unusual thought: why not dig a hole and drop in a grade school? That way, when the Russkies get an itchy trigger finger, the place can double as a fallout shelter. People at first greeted the plan with laughs: that school, some snickered, will never see the light of day. When the Cold War started heating up, and when people in southeastern New Mexico began realizing that Atlas missiles stuck in the ground nearby posed a real threat, Standhart received the go-ahead.

Civil defense has, of course, received something of a go-behind since the school opened. In fact, the nearly 380 persons who inhabit Abo today rarely, if ever, think they are in a bomb shelter. And for good reason: except for the absence of glass, there is no noticeable difference between Abo's interior and that of other schools. Abo's fifteen classrooms, built around a plaza, are cheerfully decorated with maps of South America, insect displays, reading lists, and the school mascot. If you go to Abo, you are not an Artesian. You are a Gopher.

Yet there are indications everywhere that somebody had ground zero on his mind when the place was built. The school's huge, steel emergency doors, weighing 1,800 pounds each, are seven-eighths of an inch thick. Alongside each entrance is a shower stall where one can wash off radiation. Do the decontamination sprinklers work? "You turn on that sucker," notes Bach, "you'll get plenty wet." Stacked in a large closet behind the school's cafeteria are the remains of survival supplies: mattresses, dusty cartons of crackers, sanitation kits, and dozens of drums of drinking water. What would the water taste like after twenty years? Says Bach: "Dadgummit if I know." The provisions were originally meant to serve 2,000 persons for two weeks. The room that holds them is opened so infrequently that the morning Bach turns the key for his guest, several interested teachers run over for a look.

Nuclear attacks aside, the school comes with built-in educational benefits. Having no windows means more wall space and hence
more flexibility. "This is the first school I've taught at where you don't
have to go to another room to show a film," says Trelland Tillery, a
veteran fifth grade teacher at Abo. "When we first opened," says Bach,
"some people said it's a shame the kids couldn't see snowflakes or
hear the birdies sing. Hey, dadgummit, we have recess here two, three
times a day."

Named for an oil-producing geological formation outside of town,
Abo cost $468,000 to build. About one-third of that was paid for by
the Office of Civil Defense. Construction of such a school might be
prohibitive today. While it costs less to heat Abo than windowed
schools, the lights must always be on, and Abo requires more expensive refrigerated air-conditioning. "Other cities have said they wanted to build a school like ours, says Bach. "How many went ahead
and did, I don't know. We're still pretty unique far as I know."

It has been more than fifteen years since Abo held a civil defense
drill, much less a tornado alert. Bach feels chaos would reign if such
an alarm were sounded today. Still, the school stands ready. In Bach's
office sits a curious *Dr. Strangelove* touch: a red telephone.

The hoopla surrounding Abo's opening was enormous. President
Kennedy almost showed up, then sent this telegram: "The inclusion
of a fallout shelter . . . is commendable and a necessary step towards
insuring the survival of this country." The message now embellishes
the school office wall.

More than 3,000 people came by to gawk during the dedication.
Jets from nearby Walker Air Force Base, now abandoned, flew over
Abo's slab roof. The media pounced on the school like ants after a
picnic hamper. The article that perhaps generated most discussion
was a two-pager in the *Saturday Evening Post*. Some Artesia citizens
felt the piece painted the school as a concentration camp. Indeed,
the writer quoted one Abo student as asking her mother, "Did you
know there is a room in our school for dead people?" The girl was
referring to Frank Standhart's blueprint that still hangs in Abo's
hallway: under fallout conditions, the food storage room is to be
used as a morgue.

Other periodicals were not as kind as the *Saturday Evening Post*.
The *St. Petersburg* (Fla.) *Times* offered this editorial: "That the town
of Artesia, N.M. will send 500 children to a school underground is
petrifying . . . let us hope that this experience turns out to be a damn-

ing boondoggle, a waste of taxpayers' money." Comments of that sort tended to put Artesia folks on the defensive. Bernard Ross, then the principal, responded testily that Abo was a school first, a bomb shelter second.

Still, Abo could not escape controversy. When an educational researcher named Frank Lutz, from Washington University in St. Louis, Missouri, showed up that first year to do a study on the school, Artesia went into a panic. Lutz wanted to compare Abo students to those at Hermosa, an Artesia elementary school with windows. Simple enough, yet a good part of the town saw Lutz as a meddler. Eventually, he was permitted to test students. What Lutz found was what many in Artesia prayed he would: there is no real difference between students who go to school underground and those who don't.

Some of those who work at Abo say the school's teachers' lounge is the only thing wrong with the building: the room can cause claustrophobic feelings. One recent lunchtime, as six of Abo's eighteen teachers sit in the lounge, there is no space left. Between bites of sliced turkey, mashed potatoes, and mixed vegetables, the talk turns, as it often does around Abo, to the weather. "What's it like up there?" is a frequently asked question. When Albert Bach wants to know, he often dispatches a student to find out. Sometimes Bach even calls the local radio station. "When you teach here," he says, "you learn to close your car windows on warm days. No way you can hear a thunderstorm down here." This year there have been half a dozen days when the weather has been so bad kids haven't been allowed "up there." "But it really has to be horrid," says Kathy Taylor, a fifth grade teacher. "The wind must really be blowing, the temperature below freezing." Taylor is sold on a windowless school. "Kids here are more attentive. They aren't looking out at dogs or at people driving down the street."

A teacher pokes her head into the crowded lounge. "The sun's out," she announces. "I saw a fly buzzing around in here," adds another teacher. "Can't imagine how it got down here."

Few can imagine how or why Abo's roof began leaking ten years ago. But it did, and it still does. Tiny water stains now mark several support girders in the school's hallway. "Sure, the leaks bother me," says Trelland Tillery. "I mean, couldn't radiation come through there?"

The teacher with perhaps the most unusual viewpoint of Abo is Elaine Bonds. In 1962, Bonds was a student in the school's inaugural first grade class. Two years ago she returned to Abo to teach. She has vague memories of a civil defense drill, when the school was turned into a blackened tomb, and students were ordered to wear plastic identification bracelets. Bonds also recalls the criticism. "One article that came out my mother hid from me. It said that any kid who went to Abo would grow up to become a mole. My mom was afraid if I saw that article I wouldn't want to go to school. But I did, and I'm glad."

According to Bach, no child has ever asked to be transferred from Abo. It's believed that some years ago one family, fearing the alleged "mole psychology," moved across town to another school district. "Everybody I've known who has ever gone or taught here," offers Bach, "remembers it as a good experience. The people who say bad things about Abo, well, dadgummit, they turn out to be ones who have never ever been down here."

If the Abo Gophers are known for anything, it might be their logic. Last year, Eric Schiel attended school in Pennsylvania. This year he is an Abo first grader. When asked how he likes school beneath the earth, Eric answers, rather rationally, "If this school had windows, I wouldn't be able to see out of them."

Semicolon

Truck drivers call them straight shots. Tourists call them boring. And cows call the land alongside them home. Whatever they're known by, they are relentlessly long and monotonously flat stretches of highway: no stops, no scenery, no nothing. Just plain plains where radio reception dies painfully and overheating occurs often; where eyelids grow heavy and bladders cry out.

If a contest were held to decide the bleakest piece of highway in New Mexico, several roads could be entered: U.S. 54 between Alamogordo and El Paso; U.S. 70 between Roswell and Portales; Interstate 10 between Lordsburg and Las Cruces; N.M. 44 between Bernalillo and Farmington. All instill ennui. Yet all are runners-up. The winner? An almost 100-mile-long straight line between Vaughn and Roswell. If you've ever driven it and can still think straight enough to count to fifty afterward, then you have accomplished something.

U.S. 285, the two-lane blacktop connecting Vaughn and Roswell, is almost seventy-five years old. In its lifetime, travelers have wished again and again for a less tedious route. But that's like wishing for a balmy time in the Arctic. Unless you favor grama grass, this hunk of highway offers little to look at. Outside of some disconsolate cattle, cholla cactus, and 400,000 fence posts, life is limited along this por-

tion of 285. In fact, a motorist begins to look forward to the occasional "litter barrel 1,000 feet" signs.

What you encounter on this stretch of U.S. 285 is two curves
and one stop. Ramon, thirty-two miles south of Vaughn and sixty-
five miles north of Roswell, is the semicolon along this run-on sen-
tence. Blink, and you miss it. Reach for the cigarette lighter, and it's
gone. Jiggle the radio dial, and you've passed it.

"I thought I'd try and see if I liked it," says Ron Mitchell, owner
of Ramon and the place's only inhabitant. Four and one-half years
after buying the one-building community, Mitchell, a graying, taci-
turn fellow, still doesn't know if he likes Ramon. But then he doesn't
know where else he'd like to be or what else he'd like to do, either.
He has sold cars and furniture in Roswell and done lots of other things
he won't talk about. "My age?" he repeats suspiciously. "Somewhere
between life and death."

Mitchell's caution, he reckons, comes from living alone so far
from civilization. He was on a business trip ("never mind what it
was") some years back, tooling down 285, when he first stopped at
Ramon. A pretty nice place, Mitchell thought, even though it sat out
in the middle of nowhere. A few years later he bought the little red-
with-white-trim stucco store that houses a cafe-bar. Also included
in the deal were two gas pumps, a pair of outhouses, and ten acres
that surrounded the whole shebang. An instant mayor. Ramon had
no telephone, but Mitchell didn't mind. "I like my own company,"
he says.

Business is good, Mitchell reports, though not always easy to
attract. Ramon lurks in a grove of elm tress. Tired travel writers
would say it is "nestled." No billboards or warnings mark the ap-
proach to the town. "I wanna put 'em up," says Mitchell, who moves
about as quickly as he contributes information, "but I've never got
around to it."

Most of Ramon's customers want gasoline. When you have the
only gas pumps for miles, you have something special. However, gas
at Ramon is no bargain at $1.57 per gallon for regular. Better deals
can be found inside. When Mitchell bought Ramon, a liquor license
came along with the place. He sells a ton of beer for four bits a can
and serves mixed drinks, too. Mitchell used to serve food at Ramon,
but now he only peddles snacks. He also worked on cars, but had to
let that go, too. Running from the griddle to the gas pumps, waiting on customers and calming hot radiators at the same time was

too much work for one man. Still, he'll help stranded motorists—
"This here's the breakdown capital of the world"—by flagging rides
to Vaughn.

Those who don't break down or fill up often stop to satisfy their
curiosity about what Ramon's only business has for sale. They find
Indian baubles from Santo Domingo Pueblo and Chinese baubles from
Taiwan. Jars of penny candy and bags of pretzels decorate the counter.
Scarves hang from a lamp. Dangling from the ceiling are dollar bills,
more than 100 of them, each signed with a black marker—"Abe and
Sonny was here"; "Jim Watson, Juneau, Alaska"; "Ridgeland, S.C."
"People stopping here give 'em to me," Mitchell explains of the
money. "I don't know why they do it." Isn't it illegal to deface cur-
rency? "Might be," Mitchell says with a shrug. "But so are lots of
other things."

According to Mitchell, no day passes in Ramon without a patron.
Some days, however, only a few people show up and Mitchell sells
maybe a single Sprite and a bag of Fritos. It's lonely in Ramon, but
Mitchell, a confessed loner, doesn't mind. He keeps himself company by reading *People* magazine, usually seated at a table beside
Ramon's front window. He watches the passing parade on U.S. 285—
the traveling salespeople, the petroleum trucks, the families on vacation, the sheep ranchers. To get better reception on that wearisome
road, Mitchell suggests making sure the radio antenna is located on
the right side of your car.

Behind Mitchell's little enclave are his turkeys, ducks, and dogs.
He's never scared: two dogs are German shepherds. As much as he
likes the desolate life of Ramon, Mitchell has the town up for sale.
"A family should run this place," Mitchell says, nibbling a chile pepper. "If a family moved in here, they'd knock a home run."

Actually, a family—the Panebouefs—did run Ramon for two and
a half decades. If they didn't hit a home run, they had fun trying.
Back in the early '40s, a Vaughn businessman named Carlos Panebouef
(pronounced *pan-a-buff*) often drove to Roswell on 285; he wondered
why there was no bar along the highway. Back then, Ramon did have
a little feed store, a gas station, and tiny post office. But no bar.
Panebouef, who had spent much of his life around saloons, decided
to build one. So in 1944, he bought Ramon. Panebouef, the son of a
French immigrant, remodeled the feed store by putting in a wooden
bar and booths. He brought in his wife, Eugenia, to cook. Her ham-

burgers and red chile were well known in the four counties crossed by the road from Vaughn to Roswell.

But Panebouef wasn't interested only in burgers and beer. His business was gambling. He ran slot machines all over central New Mexico. Soon after taking over Ramon, he set up four machines in the cafe there, and the one-armed bandits were seldom idle. When politicians stopped at Ramon looking for votes, as they frequently did, Panebouef dropped a wooden cabinet over the slots.

In 1959, Panebouef's daughter, Emma, took over the place. For almost twenty years she lived on the premises with her mother and various nieces and nephews. In 1977, she sold Ramon and retired to Vaughn. She didn't want to sell. But after her father's death in 1965, and her mother's in 1976, she thought she had no choice. "It was too hard living out there alone," says Panebouef, now fifty-six.

She misses Ramon enormously. "That had been my life out there. We celebrated Christmases and birthdays with all our family members in Ramon. Those were the best times of our lives." She even misses the worst times, such as the fierce dust storms that left Ramon buried under a gray cloud, the strange noises in the night, and the bull snake she once found in her bathroom. "Ramon was a trusting place. All my friends out there were ranchers. Many of them are gone now or moved away. They would take my cash and deposit it for me in Roswell. They used to look after me, check on me. When they started going, I started thinking about leaving." Seven years ago, three men from Albuquerque bought Ramon. They had the place for a couple of years, then let it go. Emma Panebouef took it back. In 1980, she sold it to Ron Mitchell.

A couple of years ago, Mitchell learned that artist Peter Hurd had once painted Ramon. Mitchell went to the Roswell gallery that displayed the Hurd painting. He thought maybe he would buy it. Mitchell figured the painting might look nice alongside Ramon's bags of pretzels and dollar bills. "You know what they wanted for that thing?" Mitchell asks, still stunned at the memory. "They were selling it for about $40,000!"

Today, Mitchell wants $160,000 for the town of Ramon. He says the square footage alone totals 33,000. That doesn't include the outhouses, either. However, until someone comes up with the money, Mitchell will sit tight. Even if a prospective buyer does make an offer, Mitchell is not sure he'll sell. "I've got things to do," he says. Like what? "Oh, things."

Fraternal Instincts

Snowy-haired Lillie May Carlin, wearing a blue sash over her right shoulder, thumps a gavel. Ernie Phelps, clasping a stick attached to the head of a screech owl, announces, "I close this outer gate in faith, hope, charity, and with fidelity."

Welcome to Grange.

Most people who grew up with soybeans and sorghum know about the dances, quilting bees, and harvest suppers held down at the old Grange hall. Grange meetings, however, with their secret watchwords and peculiar phraseology, smalt-colored sashes and ornamental staves, have always been restricted affairs. On special occasions, they're open to an outsider. This is one of those occasions.

It is a weekday evening at New Mexico's first and only Grange—in a woodchip-size community called Cedar Hill. The Cedar Hill Grange has gathered this night where it began in 1981: at the town's seventy-nine-year-old, one-room schoolhouse. Cedar Hill, a hairbreadth from Colorado, is halfway between Farmington and Durango. Cedar Hill used to be mostly pasture. Only a few alfalfa fields remain. The majority of the village's 200 residents commute to Aztec or Farmington to work for oil or gas companies.

Even with so few farmers in Cedar Hill, some residents there wanted to start a Grange. Once upon a time, only agrarian types took part in a Grange. These days, anyone can join, even oil and gas people. All that's required is an interest in agriculture. "And anyone who sits down to a meal," warns Lillie May Carlin, "better be interested in agriculture."

Also known as the Order of the Patrons of Husbandry, Grange was born in 1867 as a fraternal organization to help heal the wounds of the Civil War. The founders instituted clandestine passwords and various rituals to build esprit de corps. As with other fraternal orders, members of Grange work to complete degrees. Yet unlike other fraternal organizations, Grange has always welcomed women and allowed them to hold leadership positions. According to one old Grange axiom, women do some of the hardest work on farms.

There are now 500,000 Grange members in forty-two states. The organization takes its name from the English manor system. The master in Cedar Hill's case, Lillie May Carlin, leads. The gatekeeper, Ernie Phelps, acts as a sort of sergeant-at-arms. Other posts include steward, overseer, chaplain, and lecturer.

Grange has long been an effective lobby in Congress and state legislatures. Rural Free Delivery, the Farmer's Home Administration, and the interstate highway system owe much of their existence to Grange. But probably Grange's biggest selling point is the low-cost insurance—for home, life, car, and crops—that it offers members. New Mexico's insurance laws, and the fact that a state needs 3,000 members before Grange insurance can be purchased, have kept the organization from gaining a foothold here. The twenty-three members of the Cedar Hill Grange are affiliated with the Colorado network of Granges. In Colorado, Granges are like mountains: they decorate nearly every horizon. "We used to have about thirty-five members here," says Lillie May Carlin. "People now say they have too much to do."

One thing people in Cedar Hill do on occasion is differ amongst themselves. Take the name of the town, for example. Some residents say it comes from the big ridge behind the village. Other locals disagree and point to a nearby slope on the Durango highway. When the road to the Cedar Hill cemetery required gravel, one group in town wanted the stones a certain thickness. A second faction desired another size. But the real ruckus in Cedar Hill began when Grange arrived. Grange is, after all, a secret society. Never mind that it has little more to conceal than a peach cobbler recipe.

The Farm Local, which has no links to any national organization and which says it has no secrets, raised the biggest fuss. The

Farm Local is well entrenched in Cedar Hill. "They don't like any-body infringing," explains Granger Ruth Simpson. Farm Local mem-bers deny being jealous of the new group in town. "There's no rivalry between us that I'm aware of," says Velma McEwen, whose husband, Wright, directs the Farm Local. "I just don't care for their close ties to Colorado."

When Grange began meeting in the town's old schoolhouse, the Farm Local began grumbling loudly. The town owns the building, but the Farm Local controls it. Farm Local members say Grange hasn't been paying its fair share to use the hall. "It costs a lot of money to keep up that old school," argues McEwen. In defense, Grangers say they have given their own time and funds to repair the school build-ing's roof.

Friction between the Cedar Hill Grange and the Farm Local inten-sified when someone discovered that people had joined Grange, and had even completed some degree work, solely to report back to the Farm Local. Moles. Velma and Wright McEwen admit they quit Grange when they found the organization had more pomp than cir-cumstance.

The spying and backbiting are silly, says Cedar Hill's nonparti-san crowd. There is room in the community for both organizations. Besides, the two have helped the town. After a blaze destroyed one Cedar Hill home, the town's volunteer fire department, to which six Grangers belong, went from door to door seeking donations. When the telephone service in Cedar Hill started going bad, Farm Local members fought to make it better.

Tradition, rather than turmoil, is more familiar to Grange. Most of those who belong to the Cedar Hill Grange do so because Grange was once important in their lives. Lillie May Carlin, seventy-eight, joined her first Grange almost thirty-five years ago. At the time, she was living on a ranch north of Pagosa Springs, Colorado. Her Grange was thirty-eight hard miles from home. "You really had to want to belong to go there twice a month." Though Ernie Phelps grew up on a farm in Ignacio, Colorado, he had been away from agriculture for years. "Grange," says the Aztec contractor, "gives me a way of staying in touch with farmers." Fred Crum is a geologist who came to Cedar Hill from Pennsylvania thirty years ago. As a young man, Crum lived southwest of Pittsburgh in dairy cow country. He and his wife, Lois, belonged to Granges there as youngsters. "That Grange was a family organization appealed to me," says Crum. Children are welcome at

Grange. In fact, a junior Grange exists, with its own password and activities.

Grange works to keep its image folksy. A public relations brochure issued from the organization's national office in Washington, D.C., advises dealing with the press this way: "a plate of home made cookies is always appreciated." And Grange works to keep its rituals, despite the fact that some members, like gatekeeper Ernie Phelps, are not that keen about them. "That stuff like passwords runs against my grain," says Phelps, drawing on a Winston. "In my opinion, we don't have any secrets. I've been through six degrees, and I can't tell you what they mean, 'cause I don't know."

But back to the meeting. The main order of business this night is to honor the Cedar Hill Fire Department. The chief, Jeffrey Ray, twenty-four, is one of the youngest members of Cedar Hill's Grange. The plaque he receives this evening comes from Linda Ray, lecturer— or program coordinator—of Cedar Hill Grange. Linda Ray is also Jeffrey's mother. And the Cedar Hill Fire Department is also where Grange may meet by-and-by. Friction in the old schoolhouse has been producing sparks.

Another tap of Lillie May Carlin's gavel ends the meeting. This is Carlin's second year as worthy master and, frankly, she would like someone else to wear the leader's blue sash. Still, Grange is Carlin's life. She wishes the Cedar Hill Grange would grow, however. When she belonged to Grange in Colorado, a member had to look after a duck until that member brought in a recruit. At that point, the duck was passed on. Carlin wonders if Cedar Hill should do that—force Grangers to raise a duck to build membership.

Better not spread the scheme too far. The Farm Local is liable to make a crack. Or a quack.

Cedar Hill made the news again in 1986 when New Mexico voters elected Garrey Carruthers governor. Carruthers grew up on a Cedar Hill dairy farm.

IV

Mosaics

Hurd's People

*The ones I like best to paint are those whose lives
are spent under the sky: men whose clothing, skin
and eyes are all conditioned by sun and wind.*

Peter Hurd

The poplars still rise like green stickpins, and the windmills still squat like gray ghosts. From chimneys, smoke continues to unravel like balls of yarn. And the mountains, oh, the mountains. Some resemble bunched carpeting. Others—throw-pillow hills stubbled with piñon and cedar—really do look like faces in need of shaves.

Welcome to the world of Peter Hurd. The Hondo Valley has always been quiet, but it has been more so since 1977. That's when Hurd, crippled by Alzheimer's disease, a progressive and incurable degeneration of the brain, ceased creating. The renowned artist currently resides in a Roswell nursing home. But the world of Peter Hurd lives on, particularly in the people he painted. Though primarily known for his landscapes, Hurd also was a portrait painter. The people of the Hondo Valley were his world, too, and many survive.

Hurd came to the Hondo Valley and to the village of San Patricio in 1934. When he moved onto his Sentinel Ranch that year, where part of his family still lives, the spread was forty acres and two adobes. It is now 2,200 acres and five houses. At the center is a sprawling, orange-roofed hacienda. Nearby is the polo field that Hurd a consummate horseman, cleared from a rocky pasture.

Most of the 100 or so residents of San Patricio are the kind Hurd preferred to paint: poor but industrious farmers and ranchers. The irrigated valley is home to hundreds of apple orchards. And cattle roam the overgrazed hills.

The Sentinel, a working ranch, is named for El Centinela, a lumbering, brown-and-green mound that hovers over the Hurd estate. Below the ranch is the Rio Ruidoso, a tawny thread that first cracks the earth above Ruidoso, twenty miles to the west. Roswell is sixty miles east.

As a portraitist, Hurd was something of a primitive, with links to Grant Wood. No mere "cowboy painter," he was more a renaissance craftsman who strived to combine luminosity with realism. "I paint what occurs around me," he once said.

A Hurd subject was rarely separated from his environment. That is why the artist so often placed the land—the gold-pleated mountains that rim the Hondo Valley, as well as the region's vast, cauliflower-clouded horizon—behind each subject.

In the early years, Hurd's subjects bore solemn looks that reflected the hard life of the valley. By the 1960s, the people in his noncommissioned portraits, the ones Hurd did on his own time, had grown calmer, more confident of the future. One valley family, the Herreras, bridge both of those eras, the spare and the satisfied. More than any other Hurd subjects, the Herreras represent the kind of people the artist believed in and admired.

José Herrera, seventy-eight years old in 1983 and patriarch of the family, has lived all his life in San Patricio. He was born on the south side of the Rio Ruidoso, in the same house in which his father, Luis, came into the world. As a young man, José Herrera helped Peter Hurd build Sentinel Ranch. For twenty-three years Herrera served as foreman—*el caporal*—of the ranch. Herrera's large family and Hurd's three children grew up together.

Shortly after leaving the Sentinel in the early 1960s, Herrera took up residence in a small, olive-gray house in San Patricio, beneath the shoulder of U.S. Highway 70. He lives in that home today. In the front yard are seven abandoned vehicles. Draped along the house's eaves are forgotten Christmas tree lights. Inside, above a black piano in the living room, is a framed print of Herrera done by Peter Hurd.

Hurd frequently used Herrera as a model. When he needed a rider on horseback or a cowboy alongside a windmill, Hurd called on *el caporal*. A semi-mural adorning the Sunwest Bank building, at Third and Roma streets in Albuquerque, features in the left foreground two small range riders. One of them is José Herrera. However, the best-known painting of Herrera is one in which he is clearly identifiable. *Portrait of José Herrera*, done in 1938, is considered to be among Hurd's finest works.

In that painting Herrera is standing with his right hand on his hip. He is wearing a burgundy jacket and a Mona Lisa smile. Behind him, as always, are the rolling ridges of El Centinela. When asked if he remembers posing for the painting that hangs in the Nelson-Atkins Gallery of Art in Kansas City, Missouri, Herrera breaks into a gap-toothed grin and answers, in broken English, "I guess. I was young man then. Lots of changes."

Herrera has changed in many ways. But one characteristic remains: he's still severely bowlegged, the result of a life spent on horseback. Time has tugged at the man. Herrera's dark hair has turned the color of moleskin. Deep lines cross his face in several directions. The eyes—so clear and searching in Hurd's portrait—are clouded now from cataracts. When a visitor pulls out a book of Peter Hurd paintings, Herrera pulls out a pair of thick spectacles. He examines each painting carefully. Many, he says, he has not seen before, though the subject matter is certainly familiar. "Ah," he gasps at *Rancheria*, a 1937 landscape that adorns New York City's Metropolitan Museum of Art. Herrera places a thick, calloused finger over one of the little houses in the painting. "Mi casa." Of Hurd's *The Shepherd*, a well-known charcoal study of an old-timer, done in the 1930s, Herrera pronounces, "Muerto."

When Herrera worked for the Hurds, the foreman's adobe stood 100 yards from the Sentinel Ranch house. During the 1950s and 1960s, it was not uncommon for Herrera family members to be invited regularly to Hurd's studio. The artist, in fact, painted many Herreras. And the ones he did not paint, Hurd's wife, Henriette, sister of famed artist Andrew Wyeth, did.

Herrera's wife, Eulalia, died five years ago. The couple had eleven children. Five of them still live with their widowed father in the little house in San Patricio with the year-round Christmas tree lights. A handful of grandchildren also lives there. Altogether there are seventeen grandchildren in the family and four great-grandchildren.

Alvino Herrera is José and Eulalia's seventh child. Nicknamed "Nito," Alvino was immortalized by Hurd in two paintings. One,

Nito Herrera in Springtime, was completed in 1960. It hangs in Colorado's Denver Museum of Art.

At age thirty-two, Alvino, like his father, has changed with time. A wisp of a boy when painted by Hurd, Alvino has turned stocky and muscular. His nose has broadened. In 1960 Alvino wore his hair in a crew cut. It now falls to his shoulders.

Unlike his father, Alvino does not like to be photographed. Alvino works up U.S. 70 from San Patricio, at Ruidoso Downs race track. He drives earth-moving equipment. How Peter Hurd got him to pose defies imagination. When approached for an interview, Alvino refuses to step down from the cab of a big yellow loader; when a camera is brandished, Alvino puts his hand over his face. In Hurd paintings, Alvino wears a guarded expression. He hasn't lost it.

According to his siblings, Alvino Herrera has a passion for softball. He plays left field for a Ruidoso fast-pitch team. He doesn't, however, have much interest in discussing Peter Hurd. He says that he can't remember anything about the paintings other than that it was Hurd who handed him the lariat prop he clasps in *Portrait of Nito,* painted in 1961.

Alvino's reluctance to be photographed or talk about Hurd stems in part from something he and some of his siblings share: the awareness that while Peter Hurd has become rich from their faces, the Herreras have not. Like other contemporary artists, Hurd gained wealth and fame through reproductions—particularly signed collectors' prints—of his paintings, the landscapes and the Herrera portraits.

Delfinia Herrera at twenty-four is José and Eulalia's second-youngest child. Only a baby when her parents lived on the Sentinel Ranch, Delfinia was never painted by Hurd. Still, she is the most vociferous in an argument that calls for a piece of the artist's rewards. "Everyone has gotten rich but us," grumps Delfinia, who lives at home and clerks at Gibson's Discount Center in Ruidoso. "These paintings have been printed everywhere, but we haven't received anything for them. Sure, it makes me mad."

José Herrera chuckles when one of his offspring suggests that the family was not fairly compensated by the Hurds. Herrera says he was taken care of by the artists, just as many people in the Hondo Valley were and are still.

It is true the Hurds never paid the Herreras and most of their other models for posing. Rather, for decades, the Hurds ran a barter system in the valley. When someone sat for Peter Hurd or his wife, the subject was given a side of beef or eggs or chickens or other provisions. The Hurds did not give the Herreras the original paintings, but through the years the artists often gave prints to the family, as they did to many people in the valley. It was not uncommon for Henriette Hurd to drop by the San Patricio post office, which also serves as the town's library, and give longtime postmistress Louise Babers, or anyone else who happened to be there, a signed Hurd print. When the community's new church, St. Jude Thaddeus Catholic, opened next door to the post office in 1967, Hurd presented the congregation with an original painting of San Ysidro, the patron saint of farmers and ranchers. (The old church, San Patricio, is now abandoned; both it and the town were named for St. Patrick.)

The Hurds' benevolence, or alleged lack of it, is understandably a touchy subject in the Hondo Valley. It is a subject that is complicated by the Herreras' move off the Hurd property in the early 1960s for reasons neither family cares to discuss. And yet, the Hurds and the Herreras still are good neighbors. Some of the Herrera children continue to do odd jobs for Henriette Hurd and her son, Michael, also a painter. Both live in San Patricio.

If some of the younger Herreras are bothered by the Hurds' rise and the Herreras' fall since leaving the Sentinel, José cares little. "Mr. Hurd treat me real good," he says. Laughing, Herrera looks down at his bowed legs. "I show Mr. Hurd how to ride a horse, play some polo. And I charge him nada."

Almost all of Hurd's portraits—the non-commissioned ones as well as the commissioned—were done in his studio on the Sentinel. The room, though dusty from disuse, is as Hurd left it: a workplace of someone with wide-ranging interests. Model airplanes, representations of the ones Hurd flew as a *Life* magazine artist-correspondent during World War II, dangle from the fifteen-foot ceiling. Wicker baskets spill forth dozens of cowboy hats and boots. On one wall is a sword collection. On another is a human skull. Microscopes stand on a table top. An old guitar awaits its master's return. From a balcony where mice have been known to frolic hangs a portrait of King Faisal that Hurd did for a *Time* magazine cover. Alongside that is a miniature windmill the artist used for reference. Near a big north window, shelves sag from the weight of paint jars. Several of the vials contain egg tempera, Hurd's favorite medium. To capture the people of his land, Hurd used the land. Periodically, the artist hiked El Centinela to gather chunks of earth. He mixed these finds to make his own paint.

Not long after Hurd moved to San Patricio he began to coax into his studio the natives of the region, both Hispanic and Anglo. There came, for instance, Doña Nestorita, a regal woman whose real name was Señora Nestorita Aragon Vad. de Lar. Born in St. Rosalia, Chihuahua, Mexico, she was still warbling Mexican folk songs at age 100. There was Don Anastasio Holguin, a glowering old-timer who disliked posing. It seems the Don had learned mistakenly from some imaginative crony that his finished portrait was to be sold by Hurd to the movies for $100,000. Consuelo Martínez also was unhappy sitting for Hurd, but for a different reason. Martínez's teacher, rightfully believing Consuelo's splendid face would interest Hurd, had brought the young woman to the Sentinel in 1935. Yet in the lithograph Hurd did of her, Martínez bears a peeved look. She had, Hurd learned later, broken a date with her fiancé to come to the studio.

There were others. A sheepherder from Picacho named Leroy McKnight is dead. So are a cowboy named Bob Crosby and Wilbur Coe, a prominent rancher from across the way. A sharecropper's son named Earl Wagner, featured in Hurd's haunting 1939 *Boy from the Plains*, is believed to be residing somewhere in south Texas. Bernabé Lara, another young man who sat for Hurd several times in the 1930s, is thought to be living, but no one knows where. Same with Lionel Sedillo, once a cook on the Sentinel.

Then there was Lyndon Johnson. LBJ never darkened the studio; Hurd worked mainly from photographs of the then-president to paint what one wag called "the Hurd Shot Round the World." "Ugliest thing I ever saw," groaned Johnson upon seeing the painting in 1966. Though Hurd had established a reputation nearly thirty years earlier, the artist became a household name after the Johnson incident. LBJ may have hated his likeness, but everybody wanted a peek at it. And many wanted to buy it, including the owner of Uncle Bill's Pancake House in Saint Louis, Missouri. Hurd, as he so often did, had the last laugh. The White House shunned his painting, but not the Smithsonian Institution. It's still on display there.

Portrait of Felix Herrera was completed in 1957. The work, which shows a slouching young man with thumbs stuck jauntily in his pockets, is now part of a private collection. The subject of the painting lives in a well-groomed stucco house in Portales.

Felix Herrera is José's oldest son, and the only child in the family to attend college. Felix left the valley in 1969, moving first to Roswell, then to Portales, where he and his wife, Monica, enrolled at

Eastern New Mexico University. Felix never received a degree; he now works as a carpenter. Monica Herrera, however, graduated and is a recruiter for ENMU.

Felix was fifteen and a sophomore at Hondo High School when Hurd called him to his studio. Of all the Herreras captured by the artist, Felix seems to have changed the least; at age forty-two, he has the handsome, dark countenance of a middle-aged matador.

The portrait sessions, says Felix, were done after school and on weekends. About them Felix remembers one thing, trivial then but significant now because it truly identifies the work. "When Mr. Hurd asked me if I was tired, and I told him I was, he told me to hook my fingers in my pants like that."

For years afterward, Felix says, he never saw even a print of the painting. He knew "someone from the East" owned the original. It was only recently, when Henriette Hurd gave José Herrera a copy of a catalog detailing a recent Peter Hurd exhibition at the Phoenix Art Museum, that Felix got a good look at himself. It was also the first time Felix's two children, both in their twenties, saw their father's portrait. They loved it.

Felix Herrera is an ardent admirer of Peter Hurd scenes. He says Hurd painted the Hondo Valley as it truly is. Every time Felix sees a Hurd landscape, he becomes homesick. Like other Herreras, Felix played polo with the Hurds. Now he rides but once a year, when he returns to the valley to hunt deer. He goes home, a 2½-hour drive from Portales, several times a month. "If I could live anywhere," Felix says, "I would definitely live back there."

Felix's wife, Monica, who also grew up in the valley, pines for home, too. She is, she believes, the only Herrera with a working knowledge of art. Because her job with ENMU is stress-filled, she paints in her spare time, and she has taken lessons at the college. Several of Monica's landscapes decorate the Herreras' Portales home.

When asked if it bothers him that he hasn't received anything from his Peter Hurd portrait, Felix Herrera shrugs. His wife offers a story, however. Some years ago, Monica says, she took her mother to the Sentinel Ranch and asked Hurd to sketch the older woman. The artist produced a quick drawing of a señora rolling tortillas. For a long time Monica didn't know what to do with the sketch. Recently, she had a couple of hundred copies made from it. She says she will give them out at family reunions. Would she ever sell the reproductions? The question brings a smile that suggests this: if Peter Hurd can make money from us, why can't we make money from him?

The Herrera to whom Hurd gave greatest visibility lives quietly in a working-class neighborhood near downtown Roswell. A pleasant woman who laughs easily, Dorothy Gomez, thirty-five, is José Herrera's sixth child, "right in the middle," she calculates. She is also the subject of Hurd's memorable *Eve of St. John.*

The well-known 1960 painting, on display in California's San Diego Museum of Art, has perhaps been reproduced more than any other Hurd work. Copies of the painting of a young girl holding a candle grace everything from note paper to napkins. *Eve of St. John* is to Peter Hurd what the highly emotional *Christina's World* is to Hurd's brother-in-law, Andrew Wyeth: a hallmark work.

Dorothy Herrera left San Patricio thirteen years ago to marry Luis Gomez, a Roswell carpenter. The couple has two children. When Dorothy cradles the youngest, Louie, born last April, she does it with the same gentleness she gives to the candle in the painting.

As a youngster, Dorothy did as many of the Herrera children did: she played with the Hurd kids, cooled herself in the Rio Ruidoso, and rode horses belonging to the Sentinel Ranch. Dorothy's part-time job was sweeping the patio in front of Peter Hurd's studio. She was ten when Hurd asked her to sit for him. Dorothy says the artist had already filled in the background of *Eve of St. John*: the twin mountains, the tiny horse and rider, the distant houses glowing at sundown. A blank place had been left on the painting for her.

Just as it was Hurd's idea to have José Herrera put his hand on hip, to have Alvino clutch a rope, to have Felix tuck his thumbs in his jeans, it was also Hurd's idea to have Dorothy shelter a lighted candle. Dorothy, in fact, held several candles while being painted. The sitting took about three weeks. "I remember seeing the painting as Mr. Hurd went along," says Dorothy, whose long black hair is tinseled with gray now and is considerably shorter than it was in 1960. "He didn't talk to me when he painted; he just worked. Does it look like me? Oh, yes. All of Mr. Hurd's paintings look like the people he did. He was very good at that."

Dorothy recalls meeting the couple who originally bought *Eve of St. John* and then donated it to the San Diego museum: "They were nice people. That is all I remember." She says Hurd gave her a print of the painting when she was sixteen, all the reward she ever wanted. "To my friend, Dorothy," the artist inscribed on the print. She had the picture framed, and it hung for years in her home. But the frame broke not long ago, and Dorothy does not know where the print is.

She does know, however, of the widespread appeal of the painting. It is an eerie feeling, Dorothy says, to see herself spotlighted in dozens of living rooms, including her brother's. Felix doesn't have a copy of his own portrait, yet *Eve of St. John* decorates a spot above his mantel in Portales. His wife, Monica, purchased the poster print at the ENMU student bookstore. "It is the softness of the painting that I love so much," says Monica. "And of course, it has someone in our family."

The candle Dorothy is holding in *Eve of St. John*, the incandescence of her face, and the approaching darkness around her, all give the painting a spiritual quality. The title certainly suggests something religious. Yet the sacredness is ambiguous for some. Dorothy Gomez is a conscientious Catholic, but she has no idea of the theological meaning behind the painting. The Hurd family believes Peter Hurd, a non-Catholic, named the painting after a holy day celebrated at St. John's Catholic Church in Roswell. An official at that church is sure the title comes from St. John the Baptist, whose feast day is celebrated at northern New Mexico's San Juan Pueblo on June 24 with a special Mass and dancing. The confusion behind the painting's meaning is further heightened by its subject. "Mr. Hurd," says Dorothy, "never told me why he wanted me to hold a candle."

Those days when the three Hurd children romped with the many Herrera youngsters were happy times. Carol, the Hurds' only daughter, recalls with great fondness growing up on the Sentinel. With less pleasure does she remember posing for her father.

Peter Hurd painted his daughter three times. Carol Hurd, who has her father's slender, angular features, explains it was not easy to sit for the painter, at least if you were a family member. And then it was hard not to. "I was always around; I was a guinea pig," says Carol, who still lives on the Sentinel and, like nearly everyone in the Hurd family, paints. Her specialty is horses, and she has received favorable reviews.

"When my mother painted me," Carol recalls, "she would keep me still by telling me these incredible fairy tales in which I was the heroine. My father was a man of tremendous wit; he would tell wonderful stories around the dinner table. But when he was painting me, he would start a conversation, then get bored. Posing for him wasn't fun for me; I wanted to do other things. Sure, I could take a rest, but I felt he resented it."

Carol on Horseback was completed in 1950, when the artist's daughter was fifteen. As in his other portraits, Hurd had done the mountainous background first, then put in his subject. In this painting, he included a horse in the foreground before placing Carol atop it. How did he manage that? "He had me sitting in a chair, sitting straighter than I usually sit." The horse Hurd used for the painting was a barrel-racer named Locula. "We all loved her," says Carol. Locula had a colt that Carol still rides. What Hurd achieved in *Carol on Horseback*, according to his daughter, was what the artist strived for in all his portraits: a singular radiance. "He would start with a drawing of a subject. Then he would put over that an underpainting in green, which you do with egg tempera. This green underpainting made me look like a ghoul. But when he added flesh tones, the underpainting really highlighted my face."

Carol Hurd doesn't think her father much liked to do commissioned portraits—the ones where, say, a Houston oilman would, at his wife's insistence, fly to the Sentinel in his own plane to pose in a new bola necktie. But Hurd had to do these jobs: they paid the bills. When the artist painted what he wanted to, Carol says, landscapes came first. "But if he found subjects who were organic parts of this area, like José and Felix, father would become terribly excited."

Another person who has been around the Hurd ranch for many years, more than forty in this case, is the family's housekeeper, Oliva Montoya Miranda. A short, cordial woman, Miranda was sketched once by Hurd, but never painted. That honor was, however, given her father, Pablo Montoya. Hurd's *Don Pablo*, done in tempera in 1961, belongs to Hallmark Cards in Kansas City, Missouri.

A rancher at Arabela for many years, as well as janitor at the San Patricio School, Pablo Montoya died in 1969 at age seventy-four. His daughter says her father never saw his painting. She owns a charcoal rendering of the portrait. However, it was only a few years ago that she saw for the first time the original. It came to the Roswell Museum and Art Center as part of a traveling show. "Oh, it just moved me," Miranda sighs. "I remember thinking, 'I wish I had thousands and thousands of dollars. I would buy it.' "

Gerald Marr has seen two different Hurd paintings of himself in profile in two different museums: the Lincoln courthouse in Lincoln and the Fine Arts Museum in Colorado Springs, Colorado.

It was 1953 when Marr, then a blond fifteen-year-old with a thirst for rodeoing, was painted by Hurd. The portrait session was the result of a prize. As the winner of the all-around junior title at the Billy the

Kid Rodeo in Lincoln, Marr earned a trip to New York City, a new saddle, and the opportunity to sit for Peter Hurd. "Sure, I knew who he was," says Marr, who today lives in Tularosa. "Everybody in our part of the world knew Peter Hurd."

When *Gerald Marr* was finished, it went on tour. "I'm not trying to brag," says Marr, "but, man, everybody liked that painting. It won a slew of prizes." Hurd liked the portrait so much that he asked Marr to pose again. The result was a replica of the first painting. The two *Gerald Marr* pictures appear almost identical. "You have to get up real close to tell one from the other," says the man who should know. Lean and likeable, Marr at forty-five resembles a young Roy Rogers. He looks, in fact, as if he could still ride bulls. But he has quit rodeoing; he now trains race horses at the same track where Alvino Herrera works.

When Marr and his wife, Charlene, were married, friends gave the couple a signed print of *Gerald Marr*. Marr can't remember if it's the first or second version. For the first *Gerald Marr*, the subject posed for the thrill of it all. For the second painting, he was paid five dollars by Hurd. "I've still got the money," Marr confesses. "That was one check I never wanted to cash."

Of all the portraits he did, the one Hurd likes best, according to his wife, is *El Mocho*, an egg tempera on panel. Hurd completed it in 1936, early in his career. It won him a major award and enough prize money to give the Sentinel Ranch indoor plumbing. The subject was a ranch hand named Carlos Miranda, now dead. An uncle of the Herrera children, Miranda had one of those long, El Greco-like haunted visages that fascinated Hurd. Miranda's face doubly interested the artist because there was something plainly wrong with it. *El Mocho* in Spanish means "the maimed." A strange disease had left Miranda at birth with oddly shaped facial bones. When Miranda asked Hurd why he wanted to paint someone who looked so unusual, Hurd told the laborer that if he painted Miranda as he appeared, strange bones and all, people might take notice, and commissions might come his way. Miranda understood.

Like many artists, Hurd painted himself several times. In *The Oasis*, a popular panorama fashioned in 1947, the artist and his younger brother, Bill, are the two boys skinny-dipping in a windmill tank. Hurd did the painting from a childhood memory of growing up in Roswell. Nine years after *The Oasis* was unveiled, Hurd turned out a more probing self-portrait. His face, in fact, bears a somewhat pained expression, as if he did not like what he saw. Both paintings belong to the Roswell Museum.

Peter Hurd's nickname for his wife, Henriette, a tiny sprite of a woman, is "Bean." She often calls him "Papa." Between regular visits to her ailing Papa, Mrs. Hurd still paints in her own studio on the Sentinel. Her forte is flowers. "Papa was a stickler about painting people as they really looked," she says. "Sunken cheekbones, oversize hands, ears with pieces missing, Papa insisted on including them all in a portrait."

Along with the land he loved.

Peter Hurd died July 9, 1984 in Roswell. He was seventy-nine years old.

Neo-imbroglio

It was during the spring of 1981 that Marvin Newton first noticed the painting. A slender, bearded art teacher at Raton High School, Newton occasionally visited other classrooms in the city. This day he was in Columbian Elementary School, a beige brick building on Raton's north side.

Located above a water fountain just inside the school's entranceway was a 2-by-2½-foot gold-framed painting of an Indian chief wearing a red headdress. Standing beside a white horse and in back of a mesquite bush, the Indian was staring down at a sun-bleached cow's skull.

Newton didn't know the composition, but he did recognize the artist's signature: Bert G. Phillips. In college, Newton had studied the famed Taos Society of Artists, western painters who helped to establish Taos as an art colony. Bert Phillips had started that organization.

Although Newton felt an elementary school a somewhat unusual place for what might be a valuable piece of art, he said nothing. He made a mental note, however. Some months later Newton took a group of Raton art students to Santa Fe. While touring galleries in that city, the teacher noticed several works by the Taos Society of Artists—men like Ernest Blumenschein, Oscar Berninghaus, and, of course, Bert Phillips. Newton noticed something else: paintings by those artists often bore price tags that went as high as $75,000.

At that point Newton realized the painting in Columbian School was no trifle. A few weeks later he mentioned that fact to Russell Knudson, superintendent of Raton schools. Knudson listened but, like other people in Raton, he couldn't see great worth in a piece of art that had literally been hanging around for years.

But Marv Newton is a persistent fellow. After being prodded by him several more times, Knudson decided to investigate. In October 1981, the superintendent, Newton, and Leonard Hays, principal of Raton High School, were scheduled to go to Santa Fe to interview a prospective candidate for Raton's artist-in-the-schools program. They decided to take along the painting. When they removed the canvas from Columbian's wall, Knudson and Newton discovered some yellowed papers fastened to the back. One was a handwritten letter postmarked Taos and dated June 17, 1920. From Bert Phillips, the message was addressed to Columbian's then-principal, Florence Oliver. The note thanked Oliver for "the check on final settlement for the picture" which the artist identified as *The Last Trail*.

In Santa Fe, the three Raton educators carried *The Last Trail* to the Fenn Galleries, one of New Mexico's largest art emporiums. Forrest Fenn, a well-known appraiser of western art, was not in. A Fenn associate, however, took one look at the painting and said, "That's probably worth at least $40,000." The Raton men were stunned, all except Newton, who felt vindicated. "Up until that point," Newton says, "nobody really believed me when I said the painting was valuable."

Returning to Raton, Knudson, who had now made himself de facto keeper of the painting, placed *The Last Trail* in the school administration building's vault.

Raton is a small town. With a population of 8,500, news travels fast. When an editorial about the painting's existence appeared in the *Raton Range*, the town's daily newspaper, a cause célèbre was born. The editorial, which explored selling the painting, ignited a blaze of letters to the editor, such as the one that began, "Some things are worth more than money."

The flare-up became a full-fledged bonfire following another trip to Santa Fe in early December 1981. This time Russell Knudson traveled alone with the painting to the state capital. He had an appointment with Forrest Fenn.

A great admirer and scholar of Bert Phillips, Fenn recognized the painting immediately; in fact, he owned the photograph the artist used to paint the work from. *One Man's Meat*, Fenn called the painting. Sorry, said Knudson, pulling out Phillips's letter to Oliver. Studying the note, Fenn nodded. A few moments later he put a value on *The Last Trail*: $95,000. "And if you get it cleaned, maybe fix the chips on the frame," Fenn added, "it could be worth $105,000."

Knudson was so shocked at Fenn's words he barely remembers the ride home to Raton. *The Last Trail*, Knudson decided, could no longer be stored in the administration building. It needed a safer home. It would be placed in Raton's First National Bank vault. Before doing that, Knudson had the Don Arthur Agency in Raton insure *The Last Trail* for $95,000.

Transferring a heavily insured painting, which had hung quietly on a school wall for more than sixty years, to a bank vault was for many in Raton like finding out one's neighbor is from another planet. At the January meeting of the Raton School Board, the painting was a topic of discussion, as it has been at several meetings since. The talk has always been part bafflement, part disgruntlement.

To compound the indecision, petitions of all sorts have been circulated in town. School board members have been buttonholed regularly on Raton streets, telephoned late at night, and burdened with opinions about the future of the painting. Two camps have emerged: those who believe *The Last Trail* should be sold and those who believe the town should keep it. The battle is Money versus Art.

Heading one side of this artistic war is big, blond Russell Knudson. Originally from tiny Farley, Knudson has directed the Raton school system since 1972. Despite being a man who likes challenges, Knudson feels uneasy about the painting. "Sometimes," he muses, "I wish we'd just left that sonofagun where it was."

Raton has three elementary schools, a middle school, and a high school. The average salary of the town's 105 teachers is $21,814. The school system has an annual budget of $4.5 million, but it is not destitute. "We're in good shape," offers Knudson. Even so, he is in favor of selling the painting. "It would be foolish to say we couldn't use the money. The high school needs a room or two: there's remodeling to be done. We could name one of the rooms after Mrs. Oliver. Put up a plaque or something."

If it were his choice, which it's not, Knudson would unload the painting immediately. "I never thought it was so hot," he says. Knudson even has a buyer. When word spread of *The Last Trail*'s value, an El Paso woman called the superintendent and said whatever figure Raton was offered, she would top.

In agreement with Knudson is Jim Roper, brash owner of radio station KRTN. Roper attended Columbian School for three years. When the worth of the painting was announced, Roper, like some others who had looked at it for years, cried, "That ol' thing?"

"My stance is not popular with the older ladies in tennis shoes," says Roper. "But I think the painting should be sold. Why not get a print and hang that in Columbian?" Though Roper says he never took an art appreciation course, he does collect western paintings. He wouldn't want to own *The Last Trail*, the real thing or a copy. He laughs when asked why. "Well, I've always kinda thought the Indian chief was peeing behind that bush."

Roper believes there is no place in Raton where the painting, now that its value has been revealed, could be placed without fear. He says that years ago someone broke into Columbian School and threw ink on one wall, just missing *The Last Trail* by inches. Roper admits occasionally thinking it might have been better if a little ink had hit the painting. "We wouldn't have us such a fuss here then, would we?"

The group opposing the Knudson-Roper faction is led by two elderly women, tough ladies who don't happen to wear tennis shoes. Eddie Schmidt and Marjorie Leason have lived in Raton since close to the beginning of the century. Schmidt's father was once super-intendent of Raton schools. She grew up knowing Florence Oliver and Bert Phillips. The artist, who died in 1956, used to travel through Raton frequently. "I like Mr. Knudson," says Schmidt. "We belong to the same church. But when I heard he wanted to sell the painting, I wanted to lay him out in a nightgown!" Schmidt has fought for paintings before. When she learned the Raton Country Club was con-sidering selling a painting that it had been given, she raced to a club meeting and spoke her mind. "I stopped them right in their tracks."

Perhaps no one in Raton has as strong emotional ties to *The Last Trail* as Marge Leason. For nearly thirty years, Leason was principal of Columbian School. Before that she was a teacher there for sixteen years. When the original Columbian School was torn down, Leason was in charge of selecting the painting's new resting spot—above the water fountain in the new school. "I was thunderstruck when I heard people wanted the painting sold," she says. "That painting was a gift from Mrs. Oliver to Columbian School. Since when do you sell a gift?"

The painting may have been a gift, but nowhere does it say gifts must be universally enjoyed. This is part of Raton's problem. Forrest

Fenn labels *The Last Trail* "not great Bert Phillips but important Bert Phillips." Nash Gennaro, a retired Columbian School teacher, hesitates to be so kind. "I looked at that painting for twenty-some years and it never appealed to me," says Gennaro. "The thing has no color to it."

Just who was Bert Phillips, and why has his handiwork gotten Raton so riled? Phillips was born in the Catskill Mountains region of New York in 1868. As a young man he studied at the Art Students League in New York City, and in Paris. In 1898, Phillips and fellow artist Ernest Blumenschein embarked on what has become a legendary sketching trip: leaving Denver, Colorado, they were headed for Mexico when their wagon broke down near Questa, New Mexico. When Phillips arrived in Taos seeking help, he was smitten with the mountain community.

A year later, Joseph Sharp, whom Phillips and Blumenschein had met in Paris, came to Taos. Shortly thereafter, Oscar Berninghaus, Irving Couse, and Herbert Dunton followed. Those six represent the original Taos Society of Artists, or Taos Six, founded in 1912. When other artists such as Victor Higgins and Walter Ufer settled there, the society was variously called the Taos Eight, and even later, when additional artists arrived, the Taos Ten.

Always at the center was Bert Phillips. From the beginning Phillips felt a closeness to the Indians of northern New Mexico. His paintings, like all those by Taos Society of Artists members, reflect a nonviolent respect. One story has it that Phillips was invited to a Taos Pueblo feast day, where he entered a foot race. Phillips won the contest and gained great acceptance by the Indians. Phillips may have been athletic, but he was also a courtly gentleman who painted in a suit and tie. And he was feistily independent: the artist was once arrested in Taos for not taking off his hat during a parade.

In time, Phillips became a champion for the Taos Indians, whom he painted for sixty years. He helped obtain passage of a law that protected the sacred Taos Mountain. He suggested the name Kit Carson National Forest.

One critic called Phillips's artistic style "lyrical, sweet rather than powerful." He did approximately 6,000 paintings. Many today hang in museums in Denver, Colorado; Tulsa, Oklahoma; and Phoenix, Arizona. The Museum of New Mexico in Santa Fe owns four works by Phillips.

If Bert Phillips helped to mold Taos into an art center, he also built a following in Raton, eighty-five miles away. Eddie Schmidt says the reason for this was the railroad. "If you wanted to get to Taos and you came from the East, you got off the train in Raton. Bert Phillips was around the depot a lot. So were all sorts of creative people. Even D. H. Lawrence." The Taos-Raton connection was further strengthened when Oscar Berninghaus, one of the Taos Six, married Winifred Shuler, member of a prominent Raton family.

In the early part of this century, Taos artists frequently showed their paintings in Raton's old Seaberg Hotel, now the El Portal. Several of those paintings survive in Raton. Phillips's *The Story Teller* hangs in the public library. "The less said about our painting the better," cautions librarian Betty Lloyd. "The library doesn't have a good security system." Down the street from the library, inside the International State Bank, hangs a striking, four-by-seven-foot Bert Phillips painting titled *The Indian Princess*. Some folks think it's the best thing Phillips ever did. The painting, on loan from the Joe Dilisio family of Raton, is insured for $40,000.

Phillips paintings grace a number of private homes in Raton. When the value of *The Last Trail* became known, art teacher Newton says several residents asked him to identify heirloom paintings that turned out to be the work of Bert Phillips. The exposure angered people. Says one Raton collector: "Suddenly our cover was blown. It was like advertising you had sterling silver at home."

Even with perhaps two dozen Bert Phillips paintings in Raton, the town can't qualify as an art hotbed. Oh, Raton has had some talented artists, like the late Manville Chapman, who did the tableau in the lobby of the Shuler Theater. But Raton has always been a tough place for an artist to survive. Don Partridge had to work in the neon sign business to make ends meet. Joe Sluga painted houses when he wasn't doing canvases. Raton now has probably only one artist who earns his living solely from painting. Charles "Chuck" Jellicoe is sixty-one. His specialty is western scenes. Jellicoe grew up in coal mining camps near Raton and later studied art in Pittsburgh, Pennsylvania, and New York City.

In 1958, Jellicoe returned to Raton to paint full time. It was uphill at first, he says, but things got better. A Chuck Jellicoe work now starts at $400. Some go as high as $5,000. Will Rogers, Jr., owns one. Jellicoe paints mostly on commission: currently he is doing an oil for Buttram's Plumbing and Heating in Raton. "Bert Phillips was always one of my idols," says Jellicoe from his Second Street studio.

"That's why I'm against Raton selling this painting. A gem like this is too great to pass on. Chances are the buyer will shove it into a closet and no one will see it."

If Raton keeps the painting, the question is, where? Few in town see any sense in forever entombing it in a bank safe. Paul Kastler, a local attorney, has suggested constructing a "viewing vault," though Kastler admits that might be expensive. Marv Newton says he would like to see *The Last Trail* deposited in a Raton art gallery, something Raton does not have. There are those in the community who are convinced an art gallery wouldn't catch on. Newton, who paints in acrylics and watercolors, isn't one. He notes that this year Raton merchants put up $1,500 in prizes for the annual arts and crafts fair. "People here are really getting interested in art," he says. Jim Roper shakes his head at this notion. "Most of those folks who scream for an art gallery and holler 'We gotta save this painting!' wouldn't part with one red cent."

Several persons have suggested placing the painting on the wall of the First National Bank, the building in whose vault it is now kept. Curiously, the bank already has a Phillips, a mountain landscape that hangs unobtrusively behind the tellers' counter. Those who argue against keeping *The Last Trail* on a bank wall say the painting was meant for Columbian students, for all young people of Raton. In his letter to Florence Oliver, Phillips wrote: "I am delighted to learn of the pleasure and pride in the picture, especially on the part of the children." Children, it has been pointed out, do not normally go into a bank. Unfortunately, children do sometimes go into a police station, and school board member Diana Best has half-kiddingly recommended the painting be hung there.

Another site proposed is the Raton Museum, a hodgepodge of historical memorabilia on First Street. Museum curator Tomas Burch doesn't want the painting. "It wouldn't be safe here," he insists. "Sure, I've got burglar alarms and iron bars on my windows, but someone would break in eventually. It's already happened." Burch and his sister, Emily Hughes, attended Columbian School in the 1930s. They know *The Last Trail* well. Says Burch: "If they brought it right back where it was all these years, I doubt anything would happen to it." Hughes feels the publicity from the painting has hurt Raton. "It's been sad. Everyone has become either paranoid or apathetic."

It is believed Florence Oliver paid Bert Phillips about seventy-five dollars for the painting. It is also believed that when Oliver and her husband, a judge, left Raton, they gave *The Last Trail* to Columbian School. (The Olivers, long dead, had no children.) That would make the painting the property of the school system.

Tom Burch and his sister have another story. They can recall a time at Columbian when the school asked students to donate pennies and nickels to buy the painting. That would mean, explains Hughes, that *The Last Trail* truly belongs to ex-Columbian students. Therefore, she adds, the painting should hang in City Hall. "That's where all former Columbian students now go to pay our light and water bills."

Joe Sluga, a one-time Raton house painter-artist, has an even stranger account. Now seventy-one and an Albuquerque resident, Sluga claims he was often hired to paint the inside of Columbian School. "I knew the painting well, I moved it around. I think I once sold it to somebody."

Even those people who are in favor of selling *The Last Trail* foresee trouble in that transaction. Jim Roper worries that the money received for the painting might go into a school system general fund and "nobody will be able to keep track of it." A widely discussed idea has been to use the money for art scholarships. Chuck Jellicoe feels this is unreasonable. "Only one or maybe two students a year would benefit from that."

Forrest Fenn bristles at Raton's predicament. Fenn owns part of the Phillips estate; he bought it from the artist's grandson, who lives in Albuquerque. Someday Fenn hopes to write a book about Bert Phillips. "Asking 'Should we keep the painting?' is like asking 'Should we keep the Statue of Liberty?' If somebody were to steal the painting, there's no place to take it. I don't know why Raton doesn't make prints of the painting and sell those. The whole situation is ridiculous."

Ultimately, it will be the five-member Raton School Board that will decide the destiny of *The Last Trail*. Jim Segotta, owner of Jim's Exxon, is president of that board. Though he is an alumnus of Columbian School, though he is fond of the painting ("I kinda like it; I'm sort of a cowboy"), Segotta will cast a vote to sell. Last year two Raton High School students fashioned a mural of a tiger, the school's mascot, in the gymnasium. "It's real, real nice," says Segotta. "We've got some fine young artists in Raton. I think we should use the money—heck, just the interest alone would be a lot—to help those students."

It is believed the school board vote will be close. "Whatever we decide," says Segotta, "it'll be the wrong thing."

The road to *The Last Trail* goes through the thick steel doors of the First National Bank vault, then turns to the right to wind up in a corner. A battered cardboard sheath hides the painting from sight. Curtis Keeler, the bank's president, says no one ever asks to look at *The Last Trail*. When pressed for an opinion, Keeler adds, "It's not the sort of art I'd buy for my home."

Even Marv Newton says *The Last Trail* isn't his favorite Phillips work. "A lot of people are mad at me for starting this," Newton sighs. "They say the painting was doing just fine right where it was."

On the entranceway wall of Columbian School, above the water fountain, another piece of art now hangs. It is Vincent van Gogh's *Street in Anvers*. It's a print.

Raton kept The Last Trail. *It hangs in the high school hallway, inside a protective glass case.*

O'Keeffe Country

*Where I was born and where and how I have lived
is unimportant. It is what I have done with where I
have been that should be of interest.*

Georgia O'Keeffe

The silence is what you notice first—maybe even more than the surroundings. It's a you-can-hear-the-buds-blooming silence. It's a silence in which thoughts become conversations, in which conversations become whispers. It's a silence that makes a person want to be alone, to dream. It's the kind of silence that stirred Georgia O'Keeffe.

Now ninety-seven, the legendary artist remains intensely private, the Greta Garbo of the West. Still, the curious want to know everything about her. But knowing the real O'Keeffe requires understanding her work. That means visiting her world, a silent world, and trying to see what she saw. Hills, bones, and flowers don't talk, of course. Yet for every painting there is a place—and often a face.

"Most everybody wants to see the shrine," says crusty-looking Albert Bearce, manager of the D. H. Lawrence Ranch, twenty miles north of Taos. "I been here thirty years and hardly anybody comes just to see the tree."

The shrine is the altar where the ashes of writer D.H. Lawrence lie under a cubic yard of concrete. The tree is a towering ponderosa and was one of the first subjects Georgia O'Keeffe painted in New Mexico. She called the painting *The Lawrence Tree*.

Georgia O'Keeffe first saw New Mexico in 1917 when she was a teacher at West Texas State Normal School in Canyon. Returning from a hiking vacation in Colorado, she stopped in Santa Fe. "I loved it immediately," she later recalled. "From then on I was always on my way back."

In 1929, at the urging of Dorothy Brett, a painter and friend, the forty-year-old O'Keeffe came back to New Mexico for the summer. Now married to renowned photographer Alfred Stieglitz, O'Keeffe returned nearly every year after that, settling permanently in New Mexico in 1946, the year Stieglitz died. "The world is wide here," she once said of the state, "and it's very hard to feel that wide in the East."

During the summer of '29, O'Keeffe stayed with Dorothy Brett at the Kiowa Ranch, now the Lawrence Ranch. Located in the Sangre de Cristo Mountains, east of San Cristobal, the Kiowa was a gift to Lawrence and his wife, Frieda, from Taos socialite Mabel Dodge Luhan. The first summer O'Keeffe visited the ranch, she and Brett, daughter of an English lord, explored the rugged hills on horseback. Lady Brett, hard of hearing, was a silent companion. O'Keeffe liked that nearly as much as she liked one item on the ranch: a tall pine tree.

Frequently, O'Keeffe reclined on a little carpenter's bench in front of the tiny cabin where Lawrence and his wife once lived. "I looked up at that tree," O'Keeffe wrote, "past the trunk and up into the branches. It was particularly fine at night."

One day O'Keeffe decided to paint from memory her worm's-eye view of the tree. The scene she rendered was a burgundy trunk rising to hauntingly dark branches and a peacock blue sky dimpled with stars.

"The tree's grown a little," says Albert Bearce, adjusting a denim cap that is as worn as his furrowed face. Now roughly seventy feet tall, the tree is fourteen feet in circumference at its widest point. "That's the same bench," says Bearce, motioning to a small, four-legged faded plank. "It hasn't grown at all."

Bearce, whose smile resembles a torn pocket, has been with the Lawrence Ranch since the University of New Mexico acquired it from the writer's widow in 1955 and turned it into a conference center. A century ago the Kiowa Ranch was a cattle and goat operation. Then

Mabel Dodge Luhan turned it into a summer retreat. After Lawrence died in 1930, Frieda Lawrence came back to New Mexico and got title to it. Frieda, who died in 1956, is buried a few feet from where her husband's ashes rest.

Though the ranch has been a noteworthy holding for UNM, the spread never has earned big profits. In fact, UNM officials have considered selling the place. Conversely, O'Keeffe's *The Lawrence Tree* turned into a moneymaker. In 1981, the artist consented to sell the painting, one of her favorites, to the Wadsworth Atheneum, in Hartford, Connecticut. The museum paid $500,000.

O'Keeffe never met Lawrence. Yet his blue-shuttered bungalow now guards the tree she made famous. Bearce doesn't do much to the tree except pick up its pine cones. According to Bearce, O'Keeffe returned to the Lawrence Ranch sometime in the mid-1970s. She lay on the little bench, looked up through the branches of the big ponderosa, and listened to the silence. "I don't know how important it is," Bearce says, pausing to sift through a handful of pine needles, "but she did mention something when she was here. Said the tree looked different."

O'Keeffe returned to Taos the second summer she spent in New Mexico. This time she decided to paint something well-known: the church at Ranchos de Taos.

Built by Franciscans about 1730 and rebuilt fifty years later, fortress-like St. Francis of Assisi Mission squats in a little plaza south of Taos. Even by 1930 the church had become a major New Mexico tourist attraction. Nevertheless, O'Keeffe still felt she had to paint it.

That summer she bought a black Model A Ford. Motoring to the church, she set up an umbrella and an easel and painted the mission, front and back. The rear, with its great adobe buttresses—so big yet so distinctly silent—became *Ranchos Church*.

Because the back of the church was so celebrated, O'Keeffe decided to make it appear abstract. "I had to create an equivalent for what I felt about what I was looking at—not copy it," she wrote of the painting that now hangs in the Metropolitan Museum of Art, New York City.

Ranchos Church inspired Suzanne Fauser to settle within fifty feet of the famed church. More incongruous neighbors would be hard to imagine. On one side of the street is St. Francis of Assisi Mission, two centuries old. On the other side is Suzanne Fauser, a woman sporting engraved orchids on her chest.

As a young high school art teacher and watercolorist, Fauser read a biography of Georgia O'Keeffe. "It made a very big impression on me. O'Keeffe stood out for me as a female role model, a woman of great independence, and, of course, as an artist." Indeed, one of Fauser's red-and-gray-hill watercolors greatly resembles a Georgia O'Keeffe work. However, more than that, Fauser, with her hair pulled back tightly, and her high cheekbones, looks remarkably like a young O'Keeffe.

During the winter of 1983, when Fauser, who is originally from Ann Arbor, Michigan, was scouting a place to live in New Mexico, she pulled into Ranchos de Taos. Fauser took one look at the mission that O'Keeffe had painted and slammed on her car's brakes.

Her first act after settling near the church was to hang a shingle: TATTOO ARTIST. She charges sixty dollars an hour at her shop, Creative Tattooing. When Fauser began tattooing five years ago, many of her friends were aghast. "You're wasting your art," her colleagues said. She disagreed. "I thought all artists would be intrigued by finding a new canvas—and in my opinion, skin is a canvas."

"Why did I get into tattooing?" Fauser thinks for a moment. "I really have to say that it was Georgia O'Keeffe who gave me the courage and the inspiration to do this. After all, there aren't many female tattoo artists around." That leads to another question: what would Georgia O'Keeffe think of tattooing—as an art form? "I think," says Fauser, studying the blue and red snakes that decorate her left leg, "that she'd look on it favorably."

O'Keeffe followed her paintings of Ranchos church with canvases of crosses she spotted around Taos and south of there on the road to Alcalde. She painted many kinds of crosses: dark ones, pale ones, sunset-lighted ones. One type of cross moved her greatly: the big rough-hewn ones used by Penitentes. She became fascinated by the way those crosses would appear on a hill, then vanish just as quickly. That kind of cross became the basis of *Black Cross*, a bold rood with Taos Mountain in the background. The painting now hangs in the Art Institute of Chicago. The Albuquerque Museum recently paid a Santa Fe family $605,000 for another O'Keeffe cross painting, an untitled work that depicts a large weathered gray-to-white cross against a morning sky of cerulean-to-cobalt blue.

When O'Keeffe's paintings of crosses were first exhibited in New York City, some art critics assumed she had "got religion" in Taos. This caused O'Keeffe to sneer. "Anyone," she told her friends, "who doesn't feel the crosses doesn't understand that country."

Though Ernest Valdez has never heard of Georgia O'Keeffe or seen her cross paintings, he represents the spirit of a country that the artist understood well. A husky, thirty-two-year-old roofer, Valdez resides in the village of Embudo, just down the road from Taos. Ten years ago, Valdez, his brothers, Jaime and Vincent, and Joe Griego, a cousin, erected a cross. It still stands in vigil on a hill that overlooks a road Georgia O'Keeffe traveled many times: U.S. 64.

"We put up the cross to honor my mother," says Valdez, who lives in a small, cinder block house a few hundred yards from the highway. "It was a hard job. There's no trail up there." "There" is Embudo Hill, a 250-foot, pyramid-shaped mound of lava rocks and cedar logs. At the summit, the Valdez cross stands silently, six feet of bright white wood clearly visible from the road. Ori Valdez, Ernest's mother, died of cancer in 1972. She was fifty-two. By all accounts, she was a wonderful parent to her seven children. The cross represents her *descanso*, a memorialized resting place. "It took us all day to put it up," remembers Valdez. "But we did a good job. The wind never has blown it over."

Ori Valdez's cross is not the only prominently placed cross in Embudo. In fact, two others stand in plain sight of the highway that runs through the settlement. At the top of a jagged, ivory-colored cliff, one cross overlooks the Embudo cemetery. Actually, the cemetery is not named after the community, but is called Father Cooper's Cemetery. Father Peter Cooper was a long-time priest who founded St. Anthony's parish in nearby Dixon, and who lived much of his life on an Embudo ranch. Peering down upon Father Cooper's ranch is Embudo's third major cross—Melva's Cross. Melva Gardiser was a niece of Cooper's and served as his housekeeper. When Cooper died in 1957, Gardiser took over the ranch and had the cross erected in his honor. Gardiser died in 1983. She is buried in Father Cooper's Cemetery, along with Cooper and Ori Valdez. There is more: all three Embudo crosses were made by Alselmo Griego. He is Ori Valdez's father.

Confusion may surround the Embudo crosses, but not their purpose. Jaime Valdez says every time he looks up at Embudo Hill he thinks of his mother. "I remember how good she was," Jaime says, rubbing his dark eyes with two fingers. "I'd like to be half that good."

Georgia O'Keeffe heard about Ghost Ranch her first summer in New Mexico. Intrigued by the name, she drove her Model A that year deep into Rio Arriba County. But she didn't find Ghost Ranch. When she finally did glimpse it, in 1934, O'Keeffe declared, "This is my world."

By then, Arthur Pack, a wealthy New Jerseyite, had purchased the working ranch, sixteen hilly miles west of Abiquiu. Pack, who turned Ghost Ranch into a dude hostelry, invited O'Keeffe to spend a night in the ranch's Ghost House.

Ghost Ranch gets its name from the spirits that are said to haunt the grounds. According to legend, a family was murdered on the property years ago, and phantoms of a woman and infant reappear periodically. At some point natives labeled the place *El Rancho de los Brujos*—Ranch of the Witches.

Ignoring the dudes as well as the witches, O'Keeffe fell in love with Ghost Ranch. The silent hills—some small and rolling, others tall and spiraling—mesmerized her. So did the colors—the whites, yellows, and especially the reds. "A red hill," O'Keeffe once observed, "doesn't touch everyone's heart as it touches mine."

For four decades, the Ghost Ranch landscape—fossil-filled ridges set atop each other like giant molars—became O'Keeffe's chief subject matter. So enamored did she become of the land that she once attempted to make her paint from the ranch's red earth. The idea failed; the soil proved too sandy.

When O'Keeffe wasn't painting the terra firma around her, she focused on the clouds stacked like king-size cotton swabs. As someone once put it, Ghost Ranch is "a piece of heaven held together by a big sky." Animal bones—pelvic girdles, spinal columns, and skulls, particularly—also moved her deeply. She found the white bones all over Ghost Ranch. She saw in them a way to present her new-found world of New Mexico. Red hills and bleached bones don't dominate her world, however. *Gerald's Tree*, painted at Ghost Ranch in 1937, depicts a gnarled cedar. Though perhaps not as poignant as *The Lawrence Tree*, *Gerald's Tree* shows the terrain as it is: broken but beautiful. O'Keeffe named the painting for Gerald Heard, an Irish storyteller and friend. Heard on occasion hiked Ghost Ranch with the artist to look for a baked bone or a smooth rock to put into her paintings.

During the early 1930s, O'Keeffe summered at Ghost Ranch wherever Arthur Pack had room. In 1937, she moved into Ranchos de los Burros, to a house Pack owned three miles from ranch headquarters. She still uses that house. Her front yard is Ghost Ranch at its most typical: a magnificent vista of buttes and sheer sandstone bluffs. The scene became the focus of countless works, including *Cliffs Beyond Abiquiu—Dry Waterfall*.

In 1955, Arthur Pack gave Ghost Ranch's dozen buildings and 20,000 acres to the Presbyterian Church (U.S.A.). The deal irritated O'Keeffe; she liked Presbyterians even less than dudes. Supposedly a Presbyterian minister who once visited the ranch had greeted her with, "Hello, girlie, how are you?"

For a long time after the Presbyterians took over, O'Keeffe rarely came out of her Ghost Ranch home. The ice thawed in the early 1960s when Jon Hall, the young son of Ghost Ranch director Jim Hall, placed a piece of Zuni pottery on the doorstep of O'Keeffe's house. From then on O'Keeffe got along with the Presbyterians—though she kept her distance.

During the twenty-three years he has run Ghost Ranch, Jim Hall has kept distance between O'Keeffe and the curious. O'Keeffe appreciates the protection and in turn tries to repay Ghost Ranch. Although O'Keeffe has never been one to spread around the reproduction rights to her works, several years ago she gave the ranch a drawing of a steer's head. The sketch is the ranch's insignia. In addition, she permitted the ranch to market prints of *Red and Yellow Hills*. In March 1983, when a fire destroyed the main office building of Ghost Ranch, O'Keeffe handed Jim Hall a check for $50,000.

Curiously, of all Georgia O'Keeffe's works Jim Hall likes best her New York skyscraper paintings. "In my mind," he says, "they're as nice as anything she's done of this country." Hall, sixty-six, knows "this country." An ordained minister, he has watched Ghost Ranch grow into a booming year-round conference center that annually attracts 8,000 people of all faiths. White-haired, laconic, and given to whittling, Hall moves through life at an amble. However, he has been the ranch's driving force. Indeed, he is Ghost Ranch's biggest booster. "You don't get bored here," drawls Hall, adjusting his sweat-stained straw hat and pulling out a pocketknife. "Take the light and shadow on those hills over there. The light keeps changing all day long. You can never predict it."

A full-time resident of Ghost Ranch, Hall knows the landmarks— Kitchen Mesa, Chimney Rock, and so forth—as well as anyone. Though he can't locate *Gerald's Tree*, Hall says that a big cottonwood in front of Ghost House, where Georgia O'Keeffe once slept, was used a century ago to hang horse thieves from. Asked if he could tell where he was on Ghost Ranch if he were blindfolded, Hall sets down his knife and twig. "I suppose so," he muses. "If you took off the blindfold."

Even after she established Ghost Ranch as a base, O'Keeffe frequently ventured beyond. She would wind her way into northwestern New Mexico. On these trips she removed the seat of her Model A and worked on a thirty-by-forty-inch canvas inside the automobile.

At Ghost Ranch, she liked to paint the White Place, a great, gouged precipice of limestone and gypsum. Up in the Navajo country, she discovered the Black Place, a line of gray hills that she compared to a mile of elephants. During a trip to the Black Place, O'Keeffe stopped at the village of Cebolla, south of Tierra Amarilla. On the east side of U.S. 84 in Cebolla stood an adobe church with a pitched, rusted tin roof. Santo Niño Church became O'Keeffe's *Cebolla Church*. The artist considered the painting, now the property of the North Carolina Museum of Art, Raleigh, one of her best works.

Santo Niño Church, a side of which O'Keeffe depicted in *Cebolla Church*, was torn down in 1951. "It needed to come down," says Father Myron Uhl, who on and off for more than thirty years has served as Cebolla's priest. "The floor sagged, the walls were cracking, and the roof leaked." The old church was built in 1920. A white cross marks its grave. Fifty yards north, perched silently on a windswept knoll, is the newer, slightly larger Santo Niño Church.

Uhl, a sixty-four-year-old Franciscan with a face like a Düsseldorf train conductor's, helped build the new church in 1947, the year he came to Rio Arriba County from Cincinnati, Ohio. When the priest arrived, he spoke English with a German accent. He now speaks Spanish with a German accent. "I can cuss in lots of languages," he says, lighting a Camel cigarette.

Cebolla, with forty families now, is not a wealthy community. O'Keeffe recalled that life in the little town was difficult. "I wouldn't call the people here poor," says Uhl. "I don't think any of them are hungry."

Much of the food in Cebolla comes from the area's cattle and sheep ranches. Local gardens provide produce. Still, Uhl says, the town is going downhill. "Young people don't come here. And those who are here leave." Serving those who stay are a tiny grocery store, a post office, and a Conoco station. And, of course, Santo Niño Church.

The church is named for a small boy who appeared to indigent farmers. The old church, the one O'Keeffe painted, was established as a mission church. The new Santo Niño is still a mission. Uhl's base is Tierra Amarilla, but he serves four churches in the county. Mass at Santo Niño—one week it's in English and the next week in Spanish—usually lasts forty-five minutes. "Fifty minutes," offers Uhl, "if I feel like preaching."

Uhl says he's lucky if seventy-five people show up. But a small crowd does not mean Cebolla is poor in spirit. "The whole concept of culture here is based on religion." The religious commitment of Cebolla reappears every summer when the village holds its fiesta. A Mass in the new church kicks off the fiesta, followed by the announcement of the new *mayordomo*, or church manager. The mayordomo rings the church bell and turns on the heat in the winter. In the old Santo Niño Church, the mayordomo had to chop wood and light a big stove.

The new church is more modern, thanks in great part to Uhl. Hoisting railroad ties and mixing stucco, Uhl built most of the new church single-handedly. Uhl would like to replace the new church's roof; its shingles are deteriorating. Still, the new church has worn well. "One thing about stucco," says Uhl, reaching for another Camel, "is that it covers a multitude of sins."

A favorite O'Keeffe motif—second to a cow's cranium, perhaps— is a mesa with a tilted top. The hill is Cerro Pedernal. Though not particularly tall—Pedernal stands 9,499 feet—the mountain is a reference point, visible for many miles due to its distinctive shape. Erosion has filed the Pedernal's volcanic cap into a swollen thumb.

Because O'Keeffe could see the Pedernal from her front yard at Ghost Ranch, fifteen miles to the north, the artist painted the silent mountain often. Sometimes she added flowers and skulls to her work. In *Pedernal and Red Hills*, she added a favorite foreground. Perhaps her most famous painting featuring the Pedernal is *Ladder to the Moon*, a surrealistic vision of a stairway floating in a turquoise sky. Anchoring the bottom of that work is the swollen thumb mesa. "It's my private mountain," she once joked. "It belongs to me. God told me if I painted it enough, I could have it."

Actually, the mountain belongs to the U.S. government. Cerro Pedernal sits in the Santa Fe National Forest. If any citizens can claim the mesa, it is the residents of Youngsville, a nearby village. With seventy-five people and one Conoco station, Youngsville is a lot like Cebolla. The main business in Youngsville is Bernie's Bar, a green stucco tavern. Bernie's big front porch, with its Hamm's beer sign, faces the western slope of the Pedernal.

A handsome, middle-aged woman named Flora Martínez often tends bar at Bernie's. Martínez was born in Youngsville. In fact, her great-grandfather, Jack Young, founded the town at the turn of the century. Martínez says that since childhood she has heard stories about the Pedernal: that the Navajos believed it was the place their legendary Changing Woman was born; that gold and silver existed there. "I've hiked up," Martínez says, "but never to the top." With no trail to the summit, the hike is not that easy. Sixty years ago, a forest tower sat atop the Pedernal, but rangers removed it because it kept getting hit by lightning.

Pedernal means *flint* in Spanish, and some anthropologists believe that many of the arrowheads used by southwestern Indians came from the Pedernal's basalt ridges. Geologists say that the Pedernal is 7.8 million years old and that the rock on top is chert.

Flora Martínez likes the Pedernal for the same reason that Jim Hall likes nearby Ghost Ranch. "It's the shadows," she says with a deep sigh. "The shadows on that mountain, they're always different."

For more than a third of her life, Georgia O'Keeffe has lived in the village of Abiquiu. Ghost Ranch is O'Keeffe's summer home. Abiquiu, a languid Hispanic settlement twenty-two miles northwest of Española, is her winter place. "Downtown," she calls it.

Though the bulk of her work portrays Ghost Ranch, O'Keeffe paints her downtown winter place, too. Numerous times she has depicted the walls and doorways of her 150-year-old house.

People in Abiquiu are used to outsiders asking about the community's most famous resident. Occasionally villagers point to the big hacienda on the edge of town. But most of the time they do as Jim Hall does: protect the artist. "Georgia O'Keeffe?" a villager may respond. "¿Quién sabe?"

Once in a while, O'Keeffe, dressed in her familiar black, may saunter through the town square. She'll walk past St. Thomas parish and the big gym next door, a building, like Ghost Ranch's new offices, that she helped finance.

Oddly, more and more visitors to Abiquiu these days seem to ask about another attraction: an Islamic mosque. During the last four years, the Dar Al-Islam Foundation has hired several Abiquiu residents to work on the building which, when finished, will house a 12,000-square-foot school, in addition to a mosque with stained-glass windows. The entire structure is being made of adobe.

Leo Garcia has spent the past year laying adobe bricks at Dar

Al-Islam, just across the Rio Chama from O'Keeffe's winter home. Now thirty, Garcia has lived almost all his life in Abiquiu. "I like the place, man. I wouldn't live anywhere else." Burly and bewhiskered, with the mien of a saloon bouncer, Garcia likes the Muslims, too. "Hey, they don't drink, man. They're straight. They're good people."

Like many Abiquiu natives, Garcia has had more than casual contact with O'Keeffe. "I did gardening for her when I was young. She helped me. She sent me to St. Mike's [a private high school] in Santa Fe. She's helped a lot of local kids."

Pausing to clean his mud-caked hands, Garcia says he likes O'Keeffe's art. "Those white cliffs are right around here. I know them, man. I know where there are some of those skulls. Right over on the other side of this mosque."

Dar Al-Islam's adobe architecture is designed to fit the countryside. The valley where the structure is being built, looks, say the Muslims who are putting up the mosque, just like the Middle East.

"I don't think Miss O'Keeffe would like this mosque, man," Garcia surmises. "I mean, she'd never paint it. The kind of things she painted were part of the land; she had to understand them. The kind of things she painted were here a long time before this place."

The kind of things she painted are, for the most part, still there— watching in silence.

Georgia O'Keeffe died March 6, 1986 in Santa Fe. She was ninety-eight years old.

Whistle Stop

Burma Shave, the stuff men once smeared on their faces, used to advertise by posting signs by the side of the road. Jerry West has done a painting that sits cheek by jowl to railroad tracks. And it, too, is causing something of a lather.

Blanchard is one of those places travelers usually don't discover unless they've taken a wrong turn. Most folks who happen by the hamlet do so from the padded cushions of an Amtrak Superliner. That's because Blanchard mainly is a railroad siding.

To be sure, people live in Blanchard (pop. 10), tucked in an isolated pocket of San Miguel County, fifteen miles southwest of Las Vegas. One part-time resident is Ray Graham of Albuquerque. Graham owns land that borders the Amtrak line. Long interested in art in public places, Graham decided a couple of years ago to erect a large painting on his property. That the majority of people who would see the composition would be railroad riders was fine with Graham, a reticent businessman-rancher with a flair for the innovative.

Paul Prendergast, an Albuquerque artist, created the first work—a stylized landscape with a cowboy, mesas, and cactus—to grace Graham's pasture. The signboard stood for more than a year. In March 1984, Graham got to talking with Jerry West, a fifty-one-year-old craftsman from Santa Fe and an old friend.

"Got somebody to do another billboard?" asked West.

"Yep," said Graham.

"Well," said West, "if things fall through, I'd like to take a whack at it."

When things didn't work out for the next scheduled artist, Kirk Hughey, Graham summoned West. "I'd always wanted to do a big painting," says West, an intense fellow with a Zapata mustache. And like Walter De Maria, whose famed *Lightning Field* guards a remote plain near Quemado, Jerry West says he has always wanted to do a work of art that would hang in an out-of-the-way place—"like under a bridge."

The billboard—twenty-four feet by fourteen feet—fit West's size requirements. And Blanchard filled his need for seclusion. The work rests on a lonely gravel road, a half-mile south of Interstate 25 near the Bernal (pop. 100) exit. Perhaps two dozen vehicles pass the painting every twenty-four hours. Only two passenger trains a day cross this stretch: at 1:58 p.m., twelve red-white-and-blue Amtrak cars bound for Los Angeles shoot by. Approximately two hours later, a similar train heads for Chicago.

Realizing he couldn't work on the billboard where it stood, West began to hunt for a place to do the painting. He wanted something indoors. Normally, West paints in a small studio south of Santa Fe. However, several days a week he's involved in the construction business. Therefore, he needed a large workplace and also a safe one, a room he could leave unprotected several days a week while he made custom adobe homes.

All the warehouses in Santa Fe proved too expensive. So during the spring of 1984, West decided to look outside the city. Because the painting would be located near Las Vegas, West concentrated his search there. One day in early June he stood before the old Santa Fe Railway roundhouse, a turn-of-the-century monstrosity and one of the most celebrated buildings in Las Vegas. Though trains hadn't parked in the half-moon-shaped edifice since the 1950s, the place had not been completely neglected. Various people had used it for everything from storing wool to making parade floats. Most recently, the makers of the movie *Red Dawn* had leased the roundhouse to construct sets and store film equipment.

Immediately, West knew he had come upon something special. Not only was the roundhouse big—an available room there measured 200 feet by 75 feet and yet took up only one-fifth of the total square footage—but also it was secure. Additionally, the space represented a natural link to the final project. Since the painting would sit alongside railroad tracks, what better place to paint it than a roundhouse?

In late June, West moved his supplies—a twelve-foot-high scaffold, a bank of lights, six pieces of pressed plywood that would serve as his canvas, oil-based paints and brushes, and an acrylic substance to protect the work from the sun—into the roundhouse.

West began by making sketches. "I'm not a sign maker, so I knew what I didn't want. I didn't want to sell Coors beer." Drawings in hand, West went to the offices of the Donrey Outdoor Advertising Company, an Albuquerque billboard firm and a supporter of the project. Donrey people assisted West in photographing his sketches. Enlargements were made and then superimposed on the panels in Las Vegas.

All summer West labored on the painting. He would go to the roundhouse on Thursdays and Fridays and work through the nights, sleeping during the days in an abandoned boxcar inside his mammoth chamber. "It was a rare time, a magical time," West remembers. "I'd be up on my scaffold, all alone, like Michelangelo." The only visitors he had were occasional pigeons and bats that slipped in to roost. At around 2:00 or 3:00 a.m., a freight train would slowly clank by outside.

West finished the painting in late August. Though Ray Graham had envisioned something simple for the billboard, West does not do simple paintings. His style—phantasmagorical, and influenced by Mexican expressionist Jose Clemente Orozco—is more often than not a response to his dreams. Intricate personal imagery and homage to friends characterize a Jerry West product.

Ray Graham may have wanted an uncomplicated work, but he liked the painting enough to throw a party in the roundhouse when West completed his task. Five hundred people showed up: ranchers, construction workers, artists, and even a few railroaders. Someone read poetry, someone else played the fiddle, and there were dancing and speechmaking. Three weeks later the Donrey company transported the painting to Blanchard and installed it on two gray stanchions in a field of scrub piñon and wild gourds.

Then came the lather. The work explodes with color and myth and symbolism: a dream painting. Two human figures stand out. One, a man who looks remarkably like Jerry West, balances atop two wild horses. The man is naked. The other figure is a voluptuous young woman. Her blue dress is hiked up. In Blanchard and Bernal, paintings of a nude man and a bosomy woman striking suggestive poses are not common. Grumblings resulted; some locals questioned Graham's taste and use of money. "The people who have complained about the painting," West says, "have misinterpreted it." West defends the work as indigenous to the area, as mirroring the culture.

Since West knew the billboard would stand near celebrated Starvation Peak, he incorporated the hill into his work. Starvation Peak, in fact, and all that West feels it represents, dominates the painting. Residents named the mountain in memory of a party of 120 Spanish colonists who, history books have it, took refuge there from an Indian attack and eventually starved to death.

The unclad man astride the two horses is, West explains, a lone survivor of the Starvation Peak incident. "I dreamed of that man and what he might have gone through," West says. "So I put him in." The woman, a cross between New Mexico's legendary La Llorona and Botticelli's Venus, is not a survivor but a favorite Jerry West image. She haunts his dreams. "I raised her skirt a bit to show she is not virginal."

The Starvation Peak theme caused West to decorate the billboard with symbols of life and death. Moons in various phases and fetuses in several stages float over the painting. A thriving cornfield, such as one found near Blanchard, marks the center of the painting. A small farmhouse with a windmill holds down one corner. A bolt of lightning reaches out from another. Skulls, snakes, and flames surround an open grave. The cross marking the tomb bears the name Tony Lovato. Now deceased, Lovato was an old rancher friend of West's. The name Hal West is painted in reverse on the cross. Hal West, who died in 1968, was a well-known Santa Fe artist. He also was Jerry's father. Anchoring the bottom of the billboard are these words: *El hombre corriendo encontra el hambre y la muerte de la alma.* ("The man running encountered the hunger and the death of the soul.")

"I did the painting more for myself than anyone," West says. "I wanted it to convey the wildness and craziness and violence within us. But I also wanted it to portray the culture of rural northern New Mexico. I love those people." West admits that not many people zipping by in an Amtrak train are going to get much out of the painting, much less out of the Spanish words. Trains move through Blanchard at fifty miles per hour. "The painting's meant to be studied. It does have a lot of detail. Picknickers would probably get the most from it." (The field at the base of the billboard is easily accessible by automobile.) Though West has yet to ride Amtrak, he says he has heard from friends that Superliner conductors occasionally make announcements when the train approaches the billboard. Sometimes an engineer will even toot his whistle.

Plans call for the painting to stand for a year. Some people have approached West about hanging it in a more public place—a stadium, for instance—after that. Fading and vandalism deteriorated Paul Prendergast's work so that it finally had to be destroyed. But West doesn't see that happening to his—even with the controversy it has caused. "I haven't made much money off this, but Ray Graham has made a sizable investment. Ray would like to keep it alive."

In the meantime, West continues to paint on a smaller scale. He wants to use the Las Vegas roundhouse again, but not in the winter when it is too expensive to heat. Wherever he paints, West promises that his work will continue to reflect his dreams. "It's a process of transferring narrative to the visual." And no, West says, he eats nothing before going to bed.

The House on Muriel Street

The year was 1958, summertime most likely. Albuquerque was creeping toward the Sandia Mountains, swapping subsoil and jackrabbits for tract homes. The crewcut, chainsmoking photographer probably noticed the sprawling growth as he guided his battered Plymouth east on old U.S. 66.

At Juan Tabo Boulevard, then barely a dust-choked gravel path, the photographer headed north. He turned again at one of the first signs of civilization, a subdivision royally titled Princess Jeanne. On a street named Muriel, also unpaved, the photograper presumably slowed to study the trim row of new houses set like gumdrops on the baked and vacant mesa. In front of a pink-colored home with brown trim, the stranger stopped his car. At the top of the driveway, in the mouth of a tar-black garage, stood a couple of toddlers, one wearing a diaper. A ray of sun shone upon the diaper-clad child.

Machine gun-like, as he always worked, the photographer, in all probability, shot from his car window. A couple of clicks and he was gone. He knew what he wanted: the illuminated child, the dark garage, a few scattered toys, dusky clouds overhead, bumpy mountains behind.

Returning to the highway, the photographer headed toward New York City and home.

Albuquerque, New Mexico, Garry Winogrand's picture of 1208 Muriel Street Northeast, has become one of the most distinguished images in contemporary photography. Leading museums across the country, including New York City's Museum of Modern Art and the Smithsonian's National Museum of American Art, frequently exhibit prints of the photograph. It's been on view in Paris and London and is now part of a show touring Europe. It has appeared in several books, been featured in countless galleries, and is prized by collectors.

Analyzed and praised, the photograph both puzzles and delights. To the unskilled eye, it seems just another snapshot of a suburban home with a Western backdrop. To art historians and critics, however, *Albuquerque, New Mexico* is an unforgettable masterpiece.

Now, almost thirty years after the enigmatic photograph was taken, two points about it stand out. The photographer gave few clues to its significance. And the subjects in the photograph grew up never knowing how famous they were.

Garry Winogrand was born in the Bronx in 1928. After wartime duty in the Army Air Corps as a weather forecaster, Winogrand returned to New York City where he studied painting on the GI Bill at City College and Columbia University. But Winogrand didn't like painting; he found working with a brush too time-consuming. "Torturously slow," he said.

In 1951, Winogrand took a photography course with Alexy Brodovitch at New York's New School for Social Research. He knew instantly he had found his field. The next year he joined a photo agency that started marketing his work. By the mid-1950s, Winogrand had made a name for himself as a free-lance photographer for such magazines as *Saturday Evening Post, Collier's,* and *Pageant.* His 1955 photograph of Marilyn Monroe standing on a subway grating with her skirt billowing and her face wearing a look of ecstasy earned him widespread respect. Two other photographs he took that same year joined the Museum of Modern Art's monumental The Family of Man exhibition.

On the side, Winogrand did advertising photography—a still life of a new refrigerator, for instance—to help support his wife and two small children.

When he could, however, Winogrand took the pictures he wanted to take, of ordinary people doing ordinary things: bicyclists in Central Park, a mother and child meandering along a New York sidewalk, two businessmen huddling on a busy corner. Winogrand would track the canyons of his native New York City and shoot roll after roll of black-and-white film. Clutching in one hand a Leica with a wide-angle lens, he'd frequently tilt the camera and then obsessively snap life's little ironies: a black beggar receiving money from a white hand; one dog leading another by a leash.

When free-lance assignments took Winogrand out of town, he'd use the trips to shoot what he wanted, building his portfolio with thousands of images of seemingly commonplace scenes. He found one such scene in Albuquerque in 1958 at 1208 Muriel Street Northeast.

The original print, which measures 9 by 13⅛ inches, was probably first viewed publicly in the late 1950s at a small New York gallery. In the early 1960s, the photograph was part of a couple of group exhibitions at New York's Museum of Modern Art. In 1966, the George Eastman House in Rochester, New York, featured it in one of Winogrand's first important one-man shows. Later, that show's curator, Nathan Lyons, included the photograph in a book, *Contemporary Photography: Toward a Social Landscape.* "There was something very succinct about Garry's vision, and especially that photograph," Lyons says. "The child in stark sunlight, the tricycle in the driveway. I remember it vividly, which is a sign of an arresting photograph, one that persists in the memory."

When New York's Museum of Modern Art gave Winogrand a one-man show in 1969, *Albuquerque, New Mexico* was a centerpiece. In 1972, *Documentary Photography*, a volume in the popular Time-Life Books series, used the photograph. Six years later, the picture appeared in John Szarkowski's photographic study *Mirrors and Windows.*

Throughout the 1970s, New York City's prestigious Light Gallery, which then represented Winogrand, placed the photograph in numerous exhibitions and sold several prints of it, usually for about $200. Another book, *American Images*, published in 1985 in conjunction with a European show, spotlighted the photograph.

Since Winogrand's death in 1984, the Fraenkel Gallery in San Francisco has handled his estate and has sold the photograph. The Fraenkel staff uses the photograph on correspondence, and each year the gallery sells a dozen or so eleven-by-fourteen-inch prints. Today, the print sells for $1,400.

A hyperactive man with leonine features, a gale-force laugh and a taste for Chinese food, Mozart, and digital watches, Garry Winogrand is remembered as an artist who never met a subject that didn't interest him. "He had," says New Mexico photo historian Beaumont Newhall, "an insatiable hunger to photograph everything."

Albuquerque came early in Winogrand's career, six years before he was awarded his first Guggenheim Fellowship, more than ten years before he published the first of his four books. Yet by 1958, when the photograph was taken, Winogrand had already developed a legion of admirers who began imitating his detailed compositions of street life, as well as his method of shooting. Young photographers mimicked the way Winogrand wrapped his Leica strap around his wrist rather than his neck. And they used, as Winogrand did almost exclusively, a twenty-eight millimeter lens. They even dressed as he often did: baggy tweed jackets and scuffed shoes, with cigarettes parked in the corners of their mouths.

While Winogrand's photographs resembled simple snaps, they were more complex. They were often little dramas built around humor, such as his shot of six people sitting on a park bench, some yawning, some whispering.

Some viewers dismissed Winogrand's world as frivolous. Who cared about all the drunken and bored guests he photographed at Norman Mailer's fiftieth birthday party? Others labeled him perverse, in the manner of Diane Arbus, for his pictures of sneering midgets and other boulevard grotesqueries. Yet Winogrand did not shy away from the serious. His 1970 photograph of a group of tear-gassed protesters at a Kent State peace rally can almost make a viewer gag.

By the mid-1970s, however, Winogrand had grown restless. He moved into teaching, first at the Chicago Art Institute, then at the University of Texas. In Austin, Winogrand is remembered as a cult figure, a sometimes gruff, other times generous, New Yorker whose personal style was greatly emulated. Not only did students walk around with Leicas ready to pounce, but they copied Winogrand's peculiar habits of developing film. For years Winogrand used the same gallon jug of developer. He'd keep a layer of sludge at the bottom of his bottle, replenishing the chemicals now and then. Soon photographers around Austin were doing the same.

An extrovert, Winogrand liked talking to students. He did not, however, enjoy expounding on his own photographs. When pressed about a picture, he occasionally became antagonistic. Usually he replied, "I photograph to see what things look like photographed."

"That sounds ridiculous but it isn't," Beaumont Newhall says. "We have to manipulate the eye to see photos, but he relished the way the camera saw things."

As time passed, Winogrand's work underwent closer and sometimes esoteric examination. Critics wrote: "Winogrand's pictures are
romantic, because they describe estrangement from the world and
the photographic imagination of reclaiming it." Or: "As we study
his photographs, we recognize that although they may be imperson-
al, they are also consistently informed by what in a poem we would
call a voice."

When presented with comments such as these, Winogrand might
run a hand through his curly hair and grumble, "Look at the picture.
I can't talk about a photograph I can't see."

Typically, Winogrand talked little about one of his best-known
photographs. In fact, originally Winogrand did not even title the image,
and it appears that way in several places.

Achieving Photographic Style, a 1984 book, spreads *Albuquerque, New Mexico* across two pages. In the accompanying caption,
Winogrand is quoted: "Most photographs are of life, what goes on in
the world. And that's boring, generally. Life is banal, you know. Let's
say an artist deals with banality."

Winogrand's first wife, Adrienne, doesn't remember his saying
much about the photograph, even though she was married to him
when he took it. His second wife, Eileen Hale, says the only time
her husband spoke of the photograph was when he saw it published.
"In poor reproductions, copy prints, you can't tell there are two children standing in front of that garage. That used to bother Garry
a lot."

Van Deren Coke, formerly on the art faculty at the University
of New Mexico and now curator of photography at San Francisco's
Museum of Modern Art, recalls Winogrand's pointing to the photograph at a long-ago symposium and noting only that it was taken in
Albuquerque.

Yet over the years the photograph has been dissected as if it were
a Kremlin code. One theory involves the specter of doom. The picture's lights and darks—the cavernous garage and the striking blast of
sun, the radiance of the child's face and the threatening cloud, the
bright house on the edge of a somber wilderness—present intriguing
questions. "You have the feeling that the photo was taken the second after the bomb was dropped," says Merry Foresta, a Smithsonian
curator.

The editors of Time-Life's *Documentary Photography* had this
to say about the image: "A child stands in blazing sunlight, limned
against the black void of a garage just off Route 66 in New Mexico.

This black-and-white contrast is repeated by the ominous dark cloud looming out of the Sandia Mountains; the tiny human figure seems to set life against the blackness of death."

Conversely, Van Deren Coke, who tried unsuccessfully to get the UNM Fine Arts Museum to obtain a print of *Albuquerque*, says, "It may not have anything to do with the bomb as it does with open land, the newness of Albuquerque at the time." Indeed, one of Winogrand's students at the University of Texas can remember hearing the photographer say that America's move to the suburbs was an important social event that had gone largely undocumented.

Whatever a viewer sees in the photograph, his eyes tend to return to the strongest emotion in the picture: the distressed-looking child emerging from a large black square. A cosmic womb, one observer calls that garage.

Is the photographer making a personal statement about an innocent tot's confrontation with a world that in 1958—as now—had an uneasy fear of nuclear annihilation?

Look at the picture, said Winogrand. *I can't talk about a photograph I can't see.*

His tuft of blond hair and incandescent underwear have adorned the walls of the Bibliotheque Nationale in Paris and the Barbican Art Gallery in London. Today, that child is almost thirty and stands six feet, two inches tall. A carpenter, he lives in Oxnard, California in a truck.

His name is Brian Sutton. His parents, Howard and Marilyn Sutton, moved to Albuquerque in April 1957, a month after his birth. A yeoman first-class assigned to the Naval Air Special Weapons Facility at Kirtland Air Force Base, Howard Sutton had previously been stationed in Heidelberg, Germany, where his first two children, Brian and Lonnie, were born. Back in the States, the Suttons drove across the country, in a Volkswagen they had purchased in Germany, to their new duty post. On the car's roof rack was a wooden wagon, visible to the right of the garage in Winogrand's celebrated photograph.

New Mexico excited the Suttons. They had never been to the Southwest before. More important, they were moving to their first house, a new home they'd arranged to have built at 1208 Muriel Street.

In the late spring of 1957, the Bellamah Corporation, developers of the Princess Jeanne Addition, finished the three-bedroom, one bath house at 1208 and the Suttons settled in. The purchase price was $10,555, and the monthly payments were $53.60. "That seemed like a ton of money to us," says Sutton, who now works for the Internal Revenue Service in Warwick, Rhode Island, and is still married to the same woman.

The family spent four years at 1208, until the Navy reassigned Sutton to San Diego. Those were mostly good years, the Suttons recall. Howard liked putting in his own lawn. Marilyn loved her shiny new kitchen, especially the gray floor tile and red cabinets she had picked out. Soon, she gave birth to a third son, Neil, and the family enjoyed many hours sitting in its yard at the far east end of Albuquerque and gazing at the lights of the city at night.

Sutton retired from the Navy in 1974. Though he and his wife made several friends on Muriel Street, the couple never returned to Albuquerque and did not stay in contact with anyone in the city. Until 1986, they had never heard of Garry Winogrand or viewed his prominent photograph. "I think it's neat, unbelievable," Mrs. Sutton says of it now. "How did he ever get the sun on Brian when it looks like it might rain? I would have had to be standing nearby in the picture, because Brian was taking some of his first steps."

Like their parents, the Sutton children never knew the photograph existed. A few years ago, Brian Sutton moved to California, where for a time he captained sport-fishing vessels. He now works in construction. His dream is to join the Oxnard, California Fire Department full time. In the meantime, he lives in a Chevy pickup equipped with a camper shell. When he has to make a pit stop, he goes to his older brother's home. Lonnie Sutton, whose shadowy figure is visible behind Brian in good prints of *Albuquerque*, lives in the same California town as his brother and works as a draftsman.

Neither Sutton brother can recall much about Albuquerque other than chasing horned toads out beyond Juan Tabo Boulevard. Brian does, however, remember the toppled trike that sits in the foreground of the photograph. "My dad ran over it by accident. It could have been the very day the picture was taken. That might explain my expression. I bawled my eyes out."

The house on Muriel Street had many occupants after the Suttons left. It was briefly owned by a black family, then a rare occurence in Albuquerque. Gloria Keane, a one-time Muriel Street resident, recalls that one neighbor, upset by the appearance of the blacks, loudly offered to erect a wall between the new arrivals' property and the next-door neighbors'. The police were summoned, a mild ruckus developed, and soon the black family moved away.

During the 1970s the home was rented periodically, at one point by a motorcycle gang. This time the police were called regularly. "There was always trouble of some sort there," former neighbor Frank Lynch says.

In 1983, after the house had been vacant for a year or so, Lynch determined to stop any future trouble by buying 1208. But when his work sent him to Phoenix, Arizona, Lynch turned the house back to Michael Maccagnano, the young real estate agent who had sold it to him. In the spring of 1985, Maccagnano and his wife, Tammy, decided to move in themselves. They lease the house and have an option to buy it.

"The place was in shambles when we took over," Maccagnano says. "There was no grass, tumbleweeds everywhere." He went to work, tearing out what was left of Howard Sutton's front lawn and rototilling the back. Buried beneath the surface of the yard were mufflers, chunks of flagstone, sprinkler heads, and other residue of a quarter-century of neglect.

The house's original pink exterior had long since been bleached to cream color, and Maccagnano left it alone. He did, however, touch up the leather-brown trim, and in doing so, accidentally painted over the numbers 1208 on the garage. Inside, Maccagnano tore out the gray kitchen tile that Marilyn Sutton had loved, and sanded and restained her red cabinets.

Despite these alterations, the house and grounds have not really changed much in three decades. The little arborvitae that anchors the right corner of Winogrand's photograph still stands. Only now it reaches nine feet.

If anything has changed, it's the surroundings. The Sandia Mountains are no longer visible from the front of 1208. A house and other pieces of urban vegetation block the once open panorama that had obviously caught Winogrand's eye. The "U" that UNM students used to paint on the Sandia foothills east of Supper Rock Park, and perceptible in the photograph, has disappeared, too.

Since the Maccagnanos moved in, their first child, Michael, Jr., was born, and their keeshond Teika gave birth to a litter of puppies in the home's garage. Maccagnano says his improvements to the 1,050-square foot house have brought its value up to $61,000.

As he holds a copy of Winogrand's photograph, after seeing it for the first time, Maccagnano shakes his head and says, "That's something, our house famous. Hey, I wonder if I could get $100,000 for it?"

On March 19, 1984, Garry Winogrand checked into a cancer-treatment center in Tijuana, Mexico. A few hours later he was dead at age fifty-six. At the time of his death, Winogrand had been living in Los Angeles, California, with his second wife, Eileen, and their young daughter. Not long after Winogrand died, his widow discovered nearly 2,000 rolls of undeveloped film in their home. Some of that film and other images will make up a retrospective that New York's Museum of Modern Art plans to hold on Winogrand in the spring of 1988. John Szarkowski, the museum's director of photography, is supervising the exhibition. In obituaries, Szarkowski called Winogrand "the most influential photographer of his generation."

It is unclear whether *Albuquerque* will be in the MOMA show. If it is, the picture of the house on Muriel Street will surely cause people to once again look at it for messages.

Howard and Marilyn Sutton have no plans at this time to attend the show; they are content to remain in Rhode Island and study the photograph, still amazed at the fact that it has given their children immortality. Brian Sutton may travel to New York if he has time. His brother Lonnie might go, too. "I diddle a little with photography," Lonnie says. "You know, birds, water, that sort of thing."

Adrienne Winogrand, the photographer's first wife, will definitely go, since she continues to live in New York not far from the MOMA. Mrs. Winogrand, divorced from her husband since 1963, thinks she may have been with him in the old Plymouth when he took the landmark photograph in 1958; she is unsure about that fact, however. She is sure about something else, though, and it may hold a key to unlocking part of the mystery behind the house on Muriel Street.

"The photograph reminds me of a certain loneliness that Garry always had," she says. "He had many friends who loved him; he was intense and constantly at his work. But there was a sadness about him, too. That picture shows it."